Redeeming Time

Endowing Your Church
With the Power of Covenant

Edited by
Walter P. Herz

Skinner House Books
Boston

Published by Skinner House Books, an imprint
of the Unitarian Universalist Association, 25 Beacon Street, Boston,
Massachusetts 02108-2800.

Printed in Canada.

ISBN 1-55896-381-2

10 9 8 7 6 5 4 3 2 1

02 01 00 99 98

Acknowledgment

The lines from "Power" are from *The Dream of a Common Language:
Poems 1974–1977* by Adrienne Rich. Copyright © 1978 by W. W.
Norton & Company, Inc. Reprinted by permission of the author and
W. W. Norton & Company, Inc.

Dedication

*Dedicated to the memory of G. Peter Fleck, who,
since 1958 in Plainfield, New Jersey, has been my
role model of the engaged religious liberal lay person.*

Contents

Acknowledgments

I developed the concept of this book, and I was responsible for its implementation. This being said, I hasten to add that I, as a lay person, enjoyed the generous support of numerous ministers during the preparation of this manuscript. It is my pleasure to acknowledge my deep appreciation for their help.

Ten years ago Alice Blair Wesley published *Myths of Time and History*. At the 1995 General Assembly I bought what may have been the last available copy. I found it an exceptionally persuasive analysis of our heritage that opened my eyes to the promise of covenanted liberal religion. It was my good fortune that Alice agreed to serve as my editorial advisor throughout the arduous creative process. She was generous with her time, tact, editorial expertise, and knowledge of our heritage. I am grateful indeed for the unstinting trust she invested in my ability to do the work well.

George Kimmich Beach's willingness to write the questions for discussion included in the book gave me confidence in the validity of my concept. His wise counsel and advice were invaluable. John Buehrens's encouragement early on was truly an act of faith in an unknown quantity. Susanne Skubik provided the blessings of exceptional editorial expertise in the final stages of preparation.

I am greatly indebted to the contributors, all of whom readily gave me permission to use their eloquent essays. And my heartfelt thanks go to all those ministers and lay people whose concern over the future of liberal religion—expressed in personal conversations and on the Internet—inspired me to complete this book.

Walter P. Herz
Cincinnati, Ohio

Introduction

Almost 400 years ago a small band of hard-headed idealists landed on the shores of Massachusetts and implanted a revolutionary idea: the free church. They formed autonomous, self-governing congregations that counseled and supported each other. Covenanting in these congregations—the process of the members learning to live together in loving and supporting relationships, or right relation—gave them extraordinary power, guided in action by the vision of "a city set upon a hill," the biblical reference for the perfect new Israel the Puritans envisioned that their community would become. And that vision helped to shape a new nation, to win its independence, to create its republican form of governance, and to serve as its social justice witness for many decades.

Culturally and spiritually we Unitarian Universalists are descendants of those idealists, inheritors of their vision. Today we find ourselves at a critical point in the evolution of our faith. For too long we have been—and are now—less a religious faith than an agglomeration of loosely clustered, high-minded individualists. We have tended to regard our tradition of congregational polity as freedom *from* institutional responsibility and effectiveness. We are individual overachievers and institutional underachievers.

In our eagerness to dissent from Christianity we have neglected, or even denied, the Judeo-Christian roots of our faith. We too frequently behave as though Unitarian Universalism was born without historical and theological antecedents. We will continue to ignore our past only at the peril of losing our identity as a religious people.

This book addresses the question of what our free church heritage means to us today. It is about congregational polity, the way free churches govern themselves—past, present, and future. It is about developing a new, inclusive, socially just vision. It is about the promises and agreements we make with one another in our covenants. In sum, it is about making our congregations more vital and our association a stronger voice in the world. It is about our freedom to thrive institutionally, to serve one another and our children well, and to serve the world together. It is about what we will pass on to our spiritual descendants.

The Unitarian Universalist Association's Board of Trustees has initiated a monumental recovenanting process called Fulfilling the Promise. Each of our more than 1000 churches and fellowships is being asked to reevaluate the covenant its members share, its bonds with other congregations, and the congregations' relationship with the UUA. This four-year process aims to help our churches and fellowships understand how better to live in right relation.

But Fulfilling the Promise begins within your own congregation. What is the covenant that binds you and your fellow congregants with one another in celebration and conflict? The covenanted congregation is the basic institution of liberal religion. Our covenant with the other churches and fellowships in our association can be effective only to the extent we first get in right relation within each of our congregations. This book was created specifically to help your congregation in its efforts to do this.

Exactly why is right relation so important? Because we are mortal; the time we have on earth is precious. As people of faith we can use our freedom wisely, in service to the interdependent web. When we live in covenanted communities of support and accountability, we live deeper, more authentic, more creative lives. The "good works" that we do are more than simply charity and fix-its; like the Pilgrims, we can create enduring institutions that implement our vision: congregations and an association of true redemptive power. Indeed, I believe, covenanting is the paradigm of redeeming our time.

The essays in *Redeeming Time*, each introduced by a brief editor's note and followed by questions for discussion, are arranged in groups addressing our past, future, and present. This arrangement reflects the sequence of discussion in a congregation when members ask: What are the most precious values we have inherited from our past? What are our most passionate hopes for a just future? And so what is given to us and asked of us now? Our past, with emphasis on congregational polity, is discussed in the first five essays. The vision of a just future is the subject of the next three essays. And the last five essays are about the present—that is, how you can combine the past and the future to bring your congregation into right relation for redeeming time today and every day.

Redeeming Time is not a theoretical treatise. It is about practice. The covenanted, autonomous church originated in sixteenth-century England, founded by people seeking to resist the state's oppressive economic and religious power. They covenanted with one another as a practical way of acting together in self-governing religious communities. Transplanted to North America, however, that original congregational polity took hold in what gradually evolved into privileged churches. Its communitarian justice-seeking power gradually eroded. For many, "congregational polity" came to mean complete freedom of the individual from institutional responsibility. It remains a misguided mantra of radical individualists in our movement today.

The contributors to this book differ in the details of their recommendations. So will you and your fellow congregants. This is to be expected in free churches. But I believe that if we discuss these differences in our congregations, we will reconcile them. Each congregation will agree on a vision and covenanting process uniquely suited for bringing it into right relation. That's the beauty of congregational polity.

Shortly before submitting the manuscript of this book, I read *Interdependence: Renewing Congregational Polity,* the 1997 report of the UUA Commission on Appraisal. It asks all of us to "begin an in-depth discussion of congregational polity" to examine "the most important but often overlooked element of polity: the responsibility of congregations to be in right relationship within themselves."

Redeeming Time is my response to the commission. I commend this work to you. I pray it will help move us Unitarian Universalists toward realization of our magnificent potential in this very needful world.

Editor's Note: Certain religious terms, whose meanings are critically important, are used repeatedly in these essays. You may already be comfortable with some or all of them. However, I urge you to consult the glossary on the following pages whenever in doubt. That way you'll get maximum enjoyment from the book.

Glossary

Following are brief definitions of some of the religious terminology you will encounter in the book. We hope you will find this a convenient way of helping you get the most from the essays that follow.

Cambridge Platform A document detailing the governance, theology, and covenanting of churches of the Standing Order in New England. Created in a series of meetings (a synod) in 1648 in Cambridge, Massachusetts, it included understandings of common theological conviction, the duties and responsibilities of laity and clergy, the covenants that bound believers to each other, the faith of the congregation, and the duties and responsibilities of congregations to each other and the faith.

A city set on a hill Frequently used description of Boston and the Puritan Commonwealth, the new Israel in the new world. From Matthew 5:14: "You are the light of the world. A city that is set on a hill cannot be hid."

Congregationalism The early Pilgrims and many later Puritans, as well as Baptists and others in the free church tradition, were congregationalist—relatively open and democratic in structure and practice. *Congregationalist* is the name accepted later by most of the Standing Order churches of New England, today the United Church of Christ. It is from these roots, primarily, that our own Unitarian heritage springs.

Congregational polity The form of church government in which each congregation is an autonomous, self-governing, covenanted body.

Covenant The common understandings, agreements, and promises made by the members of a congregation that define their mutual obligations and commitments to each other as they try to live their faith and vision. Historically, Congregationalist churches were established by covenant, a covenant often drafted by and for each individual congregation.

Episcopal A hierarchical form of church government in which the supreme theological authority rests in an episcopacy (presiding bishops). The Anglican (or Episcopalian) and Methodist churches are governed through episcopal forms.

Free Church Usually refers, in our tradition, to both democratic and non-creedal, wherein each member is free to maintain his/her own theological beliefs.

Ontology The branch of philosophy that deals with the study of being.

Presbyterian A hierarchical form of church governance wherein presbyters, or elders, from each congregation constitute a presbytery that governs churches in its district.

Right Relation The close, supportive, loving relationship that should characterize the life of covenanted organizations, as described by some theologians.

Standing Order The state-mandated, established, and supported Puritan churches of New England. Most colonies had "established" churches. The last of them was the Standing Order of Massachusetts, including several of our own Unitarian churches.

In the Beginning

Alice Blair Wesley

Editor's Note. This is the first of five essays about our Unitarian Universalist heritage. After briefly discussing the meaning of "myth," Alice Blair Wesley relates the narrative of the English Separatists, whom we know as the Pilgrims. She suggests that their story is the central myth of contemporary liberal religion. She then explains their process of covenanting and the relevance of their covenant for us today.

Wesley was Fellowshipped in the Unitarian Universalist ministry in 1978. Now retired, she served congregations in Texas, New Jersey, and Maryland. In addition to numerous essays published in scholarly and professional journals, Wesley has written Myths of Time and History, *a book that was widely used by study groups in our congregations. This essay is reprinted from the book in edited form by permission of the author.*

We need access to the past because we achieve our identity—we learn who we are—in understanding where we have come from as a religious people. We learn through stories of our ancestors, usually called history, not myth. The distinction, however, is not a matter of their differing importance, but of differing methods of research and interpretation appropriate to different genres. A myth is a story freighted with the very meaning of life. A historical story becomes a myth if it is freighted, for us, with the very meaning of life.

In the disruption and confusion and argument of sixteenth- and seventeenth-century England, we find the birthing of the immediate ancestors of American Unitarian and Universalists as well as those of the Baptists, Presbyterians, Episcopalians, and others. Of particular relevance now, I find, is the story of one particular group, the story I would have us acknowledge is our myth.

A young minister named John Robinson had been a Cambridge student and a brilliant scholar. Married, probably with a couple of children, he had been appointed to serve St. Andrews parish in Norwich of Norfolk. A fine preacher, he was attracting such crowds that many extra chairs had to be brought into St. Andrews' sanctuary.

But he was troubled in conscience. He could not agree with a number of recent rulings of the bishops and the magistracy. These rulings imposed certain doctrines and practices on the Church of England, to which all citizens were obliged by law to belong. Robinson slowly became convinced that the church could not really be a church at all under such circumstances. He became convinced that the church is misconceived if it is conceived as something done by reason of any outside authority.

In his conception the church was to be constituted, not by obedience to hierarchical authority (bishop or King), not by assent to a set of propositional statements (a creed), and not by confession of a transforming experience (salvation). This church was to be constituted by a promise, a covenant to venture together as individuals in the ways of the Spirit, with entire integrity.

In 1607, meeting in the manor house of a patron in a little town called Scrooby, the congregation formed. One writer described the event this way: "There was first one stood up and made a covenant, and these two joyned together, and so a third, and these became a church, say they, etc." The seventeen-year-old William Bradford (as an adult he was repeatedly elected govornor of Plymouth Colony) was one of this new congregation. His account includes a paraphrase of the covenant. Wrote Bradford:

> The Lord's free people joined themselves (by a covenant of
> the Lord) into a church estate, in the fellowship of the gospel,
> to walk in all His ways made known, or to be made known
> unto them, according to their best endeavors, whatsoever it
> should cost them.

The Pilgrims were, of course, much criticized for their withdrawal from the Church of England. How arrogant, said their accusers, to suppose knowledge of the true church to be reserved to themselves exclusively. They fled to Holland, spending the next twelve years in Amsterdam and then Leyden. About 100 members of this congregation were the Pilgrims who set sail for America, where they landed in 1620 and built their community at Plymouth, Massachusetts. Their congregation, First Parish Plymouth, is the oldest in our Unitarian Universalist Association.

The Pilgrims ought to be especially important to American Unitarian Universalists. They are our spiritual ancestors. We misapprehend our own identity and miss out on a great richness if we do not understand our derivation from their extraordinary spirit. I believe we could much diminish the fruitless and sterile individualism among us and instead foster together far richer varieties of authentic individuality in community if we should, through the seventeenth-century Pilgrims, set about reclaiming, for today, a fresh, dynamic commitment to the spirit of the covenant of the free church.

Individual members of a coherent free church may be ever so singular and diverse: young or old, rich or poor, famous or little known, little schooled or many degreed, liking Bach or rock or both, pray-ers or atheists, of any race, of many backgrounds, management or labor, or changing degrees of these at different times. The more singular and diverse the better.

Individual members of a coherent free church may position themselves in any number of different patterns—of office or ceremony or ad hoc committee or study group—for different purposes at different times. Picture us in shifting, lateral designs, without hierarchy. We mean to have varying, not rigid, forms of authority.

But if the whole has integrity—and a whole is a thing of integrity—the free church coheres, howsoever flexibly, around a center. What is the center of the free church? And by what power are its individual members held together? What gives the free church its integrity? I offer you this answer. You will say whether it persuades.

The center of the free church, the heart of the whole thing, is a promise of fidelity, a covenant, which each member freely makes upon joining. Actually also, each member begins again with, or renews or renegotiates, his or her promise many times in the course of the life of the church, in the privacy of renewed conscience or spiritual growth.

Too often our promise, or covenant, is implicit, not consciously explicit. But it doesn't really matter whether it is verbalized. It matters whether it is faithfully meant.

Our covenant is simply (*simply!* What a word!) our promise that we shall together seek truth and support one another as we dare, whatever the cost, to live by the truths we cannot help believing we have found at any particular time, and to support one another in doubt in those times when we can't find or can't decide what the relevant truth is.

The free church is held together by, insofar as we live by, the spirit of this promise.

I think I should put in here that when we use the word *spirit*, we speak, not of anything that can be pinned down and tightly specified, nor of anything spooky either. The spirit simply (*simply!*) is that whole inseparable complex of ideas, understanding, memory, hope, will, learned social skills, and affection, as these are actual and at once both products of and responses to reality, the results of our engagement with the world. The word *spirit* points to the interior life, which makes for the quality of our visible, exterior actions. The word *spirit* points to that with which we must freely cooperate to meet the conditions of our own fulfillment or violate our own integrity.

There is a recognizable spirit of the free church. It is the spirit of persuasion. It is both free and freeing. By its fruits you know the church wherein it reigns. I'll try to describe this spirit.

The spirit of persuasion is, by definition—has to be, can't be other than—a spirit of affection, love, for two kinds of things. It is love for other living creatures, people, and so, love for all that sustains and enriches people. And even more, it is love for truth itself, our ultimate spiritual sustenance, without which no people can long live, no matter what else they may have.

The primary characteristic of the spirit of persuasion, because it is of love, is this: It can only exist in a partnership of unforced mutuality with others. Therefore, it only uses methods proper to its nature, to freely given assent, to conviction, to the satisfaction of our longing for the rightness of sense and meaning and value. The power of the spirit may be—should be—vigorous and rigorous, persevering. It hangs in there! Yet though it may urge and press, it will never knowingly force. It refuses ever to be coerced itself, or to try to coerce another.

Yet, precisely because it is of love, the spirit of persuasion may sometimes be very angry at what—as it appears to informed and reasoning love—won't sustain, can't sustain people, angry at what diminishes rather than enriches people, angry at what is therefore wrong, sinful, deadening. The power of the spirit of persuasion can be fierce in its prophetic judgment of what must be changed for good to happen in people.

Yet again, precisely because it is of love, and because it can only exist in a partnership of mutuality, therefore, often as the spirit of persuasion is actively engaged, trying to lure, alter, move, it is just as often merely open, engaged passively, just listening, feeling, contemplating, watching, and waiting, in silent stillness.

The spirit of persuasion is hardly limited, though, to either righteous indignation or quietude, though it knows both and welcomes both in their appropriate time. Rather, it moves back and forth all the time between the poles of needful doing and mere openness. Whatever its direction, it works in individuals, as each does with others or is merely open to others.

In these alternations between doing and stillness, between acting and being acted upon, consist the famous rhythms of the spirit, often compared to the movement and stillness of the winds.

Like the rhythms of the wind, the spirit of persuasion cannot be artificially manipulated. Attempts to divert or subvert naturally arising issues and concerns, or any effort to "work" the free life of the church according to some preconceived blueprint or set of rules, is but self-defeating. The spirit of persuasion can only be worked in, as a sailor at once works skillfully with and yields to the wind. It blows where it will.

And yes, we know: Sometimes the spirit of persuasion blows up a gale that destroys all before it, and sometimes it is an equally killing, dead calm. We would be lying Pollyannas if we did not admit this, too. Every human group, including ours, is susceptible both to false hysteria and to self-satisfied or disillusioned apathy that will go nowhere. There are dangers and no guarantees with the spirit of persuasion.

And yet, as the winds hold out both threat and promises of rich reward to sailors, so do the rhythms of the spirit of persuasion to us.

So, in the spirit of the covenant of persuasion, in the free church, each member is called to give utterance, to ask, say, explain, defend what is the truth she or he sees. To be unforthcoming is to be disloyal, for how can we learn from one another without candor! Each member is also called to yield the floor with humble courtesy, to listen, be open to, and try again and again to imagine what others see.

To be unwilling or to forget to hear is to betray, for how can we receive what others may impart without their counsel! Our covenant is an abiding commitment to take and to give counsel. In the spirit of the covenant of persuasion, as individuals together we heed our call to listen and to speak to one another faithfully so that—for this is our whole purpose—singly and together we may follow what we are persuaded are better ways.

The spirit of persuasion is the spirit of a free religious people. It is holy to us. It holds all together, insofar as we live by it, in the embrace of the free church, in the generous embrace of people who are centered—in ever-changing and responsively creative ways—around a promise of fidelity together to search for and dare to live by truth.

If the center holds, if the spirit lives, there are no limits to what we may constructively do together for the sake of inspiration and mercy, justice, art, personal growth, or plain fun. So there are no limits to the difficulties the free church may overcome, or to the richness of its interior life, or to the effective work we may do to refashion and recreate our world.

I conclude with an adaptation of the covenant of the Pilgrims, written for contemporary Unitarian Universalists, covenanted pilgrims yet, in a great religious tradition.

> We pledge to walk together
> in the ways of truth and affection,
> as best we know them now
> or may learn them in days to come
> that we and our children may be fulfilled
> and that we may speak to the world
> in words and actions
> of peace and goodwill.

Questions for Discussion

1. Alice Blair Wesley says, "A myth is a story freighted with the very meaning of life. A historical story becomes a myth if it is freighted, *for us,* with the very meaning of life." Think of an example of a story out of your personal or family history that has special significance for you. Tell the story. Think of a story of your religious community (local or larger, recent or distant past)

that has special significance for you. Tell the story. Is the significance of these stories personal only, or do you see in them "the very meaning of life"?

2. What do we learn from the Pilgrims' example about what it means to be a "free church"? What is a covenant? How is it different from a contract? The term *covenant* has both sacred and secular uses. What makes a covenant sacred?

3. Why do you think Wesley feels so passionately about the subject? What is the quality of religious life or sensibility among Unitarian Universalists today that she is reacting to, and what is the quality she would nurture and appeal to? Would you join in the covenantal words she proposes at the end of the essay?

From Mythos to Merger

A Brief Review of Unitarian and Universalist History

Tim W. Jensen

Editor's Note. *In the following essay, Tim W. Jensen examines the evolving mythos of our faith traditions: What are the stories we tell about who we are? How do historians interpret the events and ideas that have shaped liberal religion? Jensen follows the evolution of the free church from the seventeenth century, when colonists created covenanted, self-governing communities, through the contentious nineteenth century, when theological controversies and radical individualism threatened to hamper institution-building. In the present, he contends, post-merger Unitarian Universalists are still struggling to merge their historical identities, to craft one common mythos, and to reinvigorate the free church tradition. Jensen received an M. Div. degree from Harvard in 1981. After earning M.A. degrees in English and in American studies, he served churches in Texas and Oregon. Jensen is currently completing his doctoral work at the University of Oregon, where he teaches in the departments of history and religious studies. He also serves as part-time minister in a small church. This essay was written specially for this book.*

Unitarian Universalism is a wedding together of two distinct and generally congenial "family trees," Unitarianism and Universalism. The weaving together of these two stories into a single historical narrative is a process of historical invention. It is a conceptual reconstruction of the past: an act of selection, analysis, and interpretation of historical "facts" by individuals whose very love of their work can bias it in subtle yet significant ways.

The recognition that any version of historical *truth* is a product of a particular historian's educated imagination can be unsettling. Yet once we get hold of the idea, it opens up entirely new avenues of inquiry. The stories our spiritual forebears told one another about their own religious heritage can provide valuable insights into the development of our own historical self-understanding. This *mythos* is the real source of Unitarian Universalism's present historical *identity* as a denomination. It is much more significant than the mere historical *facts* of who did what when. We see its influence in the hymns we sing, the holidays we observe, and the patterns by which we organize ourselves. A *living tradition* is the historical embodiment of who we are as a radically liberal religious people: what we hold in common with our religious neighbors and with everyone in the world ever moved by authentic religious impulse. It is the essential quality that gives us our own distinctive Unitarian Universalist character.

ORIGINS OF UNITARIANISM
(AND CONGREGATIONAL POLITY) IN NORTH AMERICA

On June 19, 1785, the small Episcopal congregation in Boston, severed from the Anglican communion by the American Revolution and acting on the request of their Harvard-educated lay reader James Freeman, decided to remove from their liturgy both the Athanasian and Nicene Creeds, as well as several other references to the doctrine of the Trinity. Instead, they adopted British Unitarian Theophilus Lindsey's Reformed Prayer Book. Thus, by a vote of 20 to 7, King's Chapel became the first "unitarian" church in North America. A decade later the renowned British scientist and Unitarian minister Joseph Priestley, who had recently been burned out of his home and laboratory because of his sympathies for the French Revolution, accepted an invitation from his friend Benjamin Franklin; in 1796 Priestley helped to organize the First Society of Unitarian Christians in Philadelphia. According to tradition, one or the other of these two congregations, both of which still exist as members of the Unitarian Universalist Association (UUA) today, have been pointed to as the first Unitarian congregation in North America.

One of the ironies of Unitarian history, however, is that the "first" Unitarian churches in North America are not the oldest Unitarian churches. This distinction belongs to the First Parish in Plymouth, organized in 1620 by a colony of English immigrants. The dramatic story of the voyage of the Pilgrims to "the northern parts of Virginia" in search of religious liberty is familiar to every American schoolchild and has played an important role in both our denominational and our national mythologies. Of greater historical importance, however, are the churches organized by Puritan colonists of the Massachusetts Bay Colony, beginning with the congregation in Salem in 1629 and followed in 1630 by churches in Boston, Dorchester, Roxbury, and Watertown. The realization that the ecclesiastical heritage of American Unitarianism extends back several centuries beyond its theological self-identification is important for two reasons. First, it reinforces the understanding that the terms *unitarian* and *universalist* were descriptive adjectives long before any churches actually identified themselves as "Unitarian" or "Universalist." Likewise, it contains an important insight about the form of polity, or church government, out of which American Unitarianism emerged.

The Congregational Churches of the New England Standing Order organized their society around principles of church government implicit in orthodox Calvinism, as described by the Synod of Dort, 1618–19. In reaction to contemporary "heretics" such as Jacob Arminius (who taught that God made salvation by grace available to all) and Faustus Socinus (who rejected the doctrine of the Trinity), the Synod asserted that human beings were totally depraved as a result of original sin and utterly beyond hope of salvation through their own efforts. At the time of creation, however, God had unconditionally elected a limited number of people for salvation. This grace was irresistible and would manifest itself at some point during the lifetimes of the recipients, transforming them through a process of sanctification into "visible saints."

The congregational polity delineated in the 1648 Cambridge Platform reflects this Calvinist theology. The church is understood as a community of the "elect" who have experienced "conversion" by becoming aware of their predetermined destiny. They are therefore charged to gather themselves into a community at once both set apart from the rest of society and as a guiding beacon to it, in order to walk together according to God's holy ordinances and to enjoy the fellowship of the Lord's table as a commemoration of the Last Supper.

Christ was believed to be the real leader of the church, and local congregations were expected to maintain a sisterly communion with one another under the discipline of his teachings as recorded in the Gospels. The Platform itself spells out six distinct ways of church communion: mutual care, consultation, admonition, participation, recommendation, and "reliefe & succour."

The civil government enforced public piety and morality, and every property owner in the parish was assessed a tax for both the upkeep of the meetinghouse and the support of a "public teacher of piety, religion, and morality" (who would also serve as pastor to the church communicants), regardless of whether the taxpayers were actually members of the church. Blue Laws typically prohibited activities other than worship on the Sabbath.

The tensions in this system gradually increased. In a theology that so profoundly rejects the idea of human freedom (and thus responsibility and accountability), the problem of antinomianism or "lawlessness" is always present. If grace is an irresistible gift of God, why all the efforts to practice and enforce public morality? What is the status of the children and grandchildren of believers, who have not themselves experienced "conversion"? The scientific rationalism of the Enlightenment gradually unraveled Calvinist scholasticism. In addition, the Great Awakening of the 1750s reintroduced the idea of free will into religious discourse, even as it emphasized emotional experience over reason and logic. A comprehensive account of this process of liberalization within the congregationalist establishment can be found in Conrad Wright's *The Beginnings of Unitarianism in North America.*

It is important to note that liberals within the increasingly theologically diverse Standing Order would not necessarily have thought of themselves as Unitarians or Universalists. Rather, they understood their views in terms of classical Christian heresies such as Arianism (the belief that Christ was a divine but created being subordinate to God the Father) and Pelagianism (the belief that human beings are moral agents with free will who are capable of resisting original sin), or their seventeenth-century analogs Socinianism and Arminianism. Nor would they have necessarily made their private convictions a matter of public discussion. Liberal preachers in particular tended to emphasize the importance of virtuous behavior over conformity of belief, focusing on the issues that brought Christians together rather than the doctrines that drove them apart.

In the first two decades of the nineteenth century, however, polity and theology collided dramatically in what became known as the

Unitarian Controversy. The controversy began with the election of Henry Ware, a liberal of impeccable personal reputation, as Hollis professor of divinity at Harvard. The subsequent selection of another liberal, Samuel Webber, as president of the college caused several of the orthodox clergy to organize a competing theological school at Andover. Orthodox ministers announced that they would no longer exchange pulpits with liberals, and they published a steady stream of public attacks, asking bluntly, "Shall we have the Boston Religion, or the Christian Religion?"

Eventually the liberals responded in kind. On May 5, 1819, at a newly organized church in Baltimore, William Ellery Channing preached his famous sermon, "Unitarian Christianity." In it, Channing accepted the name "Unitarian," with which the orthodox had been attempting to brand the liberals, and then went on to spell out some of the specific doctrines one arrived at when seeking the meaning of the Bible "in the same manner as that of other books," through the use of reason. The bold sermon touched off yet another round of theological exchanges concerning the differences between Unitarian and Calvinist views of human nature, and the theological lines between the two parties were now clearly drawn.

Another tangible breach in the New England Standing Order came as a result of litigation over the division of the church in Dedham. Over the objections of the majority of the church communicants, the taxpayers of the parish selected a liberal to succeed the previous pastor. The majority of the church members, including all but one of the deacons, then seceded from the parish and organized their own congregation, taking the church communion silver and various other pieces of church property with them. Since legal title to this property was held by the deacons under Massachusetts law, the liberal remnant of the church, with the support of the parish, elected new deacons and sued the departing group for the return of the silver. When the case was finally resolved in 1820 in favor of the liberals, it precipitated a spate of additional church divisions along theological lines. One common tactic used by orthodox majorities to drive out liberals was the creation of elaborate creeds to which the latter in good conscience could not subscribe. The majority of liberals, in contrast, still tended to deplore this tendency toward "sectarianism" and were reluctant to be drawn into the controversy at all.

By the time the dust had settled, there were perhaps 125 churches, mostly in eastern Massachusetts, that could be identified as

"Unitarian," including twenty of the twenty-five original Puritan "First Parish" congregations, and eight out of nine of the Congregational churches in Boston. In 1825 James Walker, Henry Ware Jr., and Ezra Stiles Gannett, three of the younger members of the liberal Ministerial Conference in Berry Street, proposed the creation of a private voluntary association of individuals "to diffuse the knowledge and promote the interests of pure Christianity"; they called it the American Unitarian Association (AUA).

Several historical themes from this narrative endured as the denomination evolved. The term *unitarian* was initially a theological adjective rather than descriptive of an institutional affiliation. The churches themselves, the actual people in the pews, understood their institutional heritage as continuous from the time of the Pilgrims and as part of the larger stream of "pure Christianity." The theological identity of a particular congregation typically followed the theology of its minister. Patterns of pulpit exchange and the issue of creedalism were also key to determining who fit where. The orthodox used creeds for weeding out liberal "heretics," while the liberals continued to express a preference for broad "covenants," which asked adherents to "walk together according to God's Holy Ordinances" insofar as one has "light to see them." Liberal theological catholicity often combined with a certain institutional aloofness, however, as many liberals attempted to remain above the strife of sectarian controversy.

AMERICAN UNIVERSALISM

The serendipitous 1770 encounter between Thomas Potter and John Murray at Good-Luck Point is the stuff of legend. Murray was an English Methodist who had come under the influence of the Universalist teachings and was then expelled from the congregation. Following the death of his wife, Murray decided to emigrate to America. When his ship ran aground off the coast of New Jersey, Murray elected to make an excursion ashore, where he met Potter while walking in the woods. Potter (according to the story) was an illiterate farmer who had built a meetinghouse in the middle of the wilderness with the expectation that God would someday send him a preacher to fill its pulpit. There, on September 30, 1770, John Murray preached his first sermon in the New World, and the rest (so they say) is Universalist history.

Thomas Potter might well be considered prototypical of the kind of person attracted to Universalism—relatively uneducated, but by no means ignorant, and both curious and vitally concerned about matters of religion. Calvinist doctrines such as double predestination, unconditional election, and limited atonement seemed to contradict an intuitive sense of free will, moral accountability, and the sovereign existence of a benevolent, all-powerful God. Unlike Unitarianism, Universalism existed outside the establishment. Its congregations tended to be small, rural, and poorly funded; its ministers were either itinerant circuit riders or "tentmakers" who earned part or all of their living by farming or in some other occupation. Many of them began their careers as Baptists or Methodists and were converted to the movement in much the same way as the people in the pews, because they found the idea of universal salvation congenial to their own views. Universalists also tended to be uniformly despised as dangerous heretics by orthodox members of the religious establishment, and therefore no strangers to public controversy.

The career of Hosea Ballou, American Universalism's most important spokesman in the early part of the nineteenth century, is both typical and exemplary. Born in 1771, Ballou grew up in rural New Hampshire, the eleventh child of a struggling farmer. Hosea was primarily self-educated and an avid reader of the Bible. He was inspired by the preaching of Caleb Rich and John Murray, but probably more profoundly influenced by the Universalist convictions of his older brother David. Hosea started out by preaching wherever he received an invitation, but following his 1794 ordination he moved to Dana, Massachusetts, where he put together a regular preaching circuit of six congregations which together paid him a weekly salary of five dollars. After writing nineteenth-century Universalism's most important theological work, *A Treatise on Atonement*, his reputation increased, and Ballou became a pastor of the Universalist Church in Portsmouth, New Hampshire; after six years he moved again to Salem, Massachusetts. In 1817 he accepted a call to the Second Universalist Society in Boston, where he served until his death in 1852. Ballou's settlement in Boston strengthened the growing credibility and influence of the Universalist movement as well. Yet what someone like Ballou struggled all his life to achieve, many Unitarian ministers assumed as their birthright. This difference, as much as any, kept the denominations separate for a century and a half.

In addition to social standing, creedal theology was another marked disparity between nineteenth-century Unitarians and Universalists. Lacking the Unitarian phobia of creedal statements, in 1803 the New England Convention of Universalist Churches adopted a simple profession of faith. The convention broadly affirmed the authority of Scripture as containing "a revelation of the character of God and of the duty, interest, and final destination of mankind." Read your Bible, the Winchester Profession essentially counsels, and you will discover that God is not vengeful, but loving, and that doing good works is good in and of itself. Around this central document, the Universalists attempted to build a denomination.

Controversy did emerge, however, although it was not quite so pronounced as that among the Unitarians. Universalists apparently came to odds around the issue of "ultra-universalism" verses "restorationism"—a question regarding whether individuals who do evil in this life will nevertheless be immediately taken into heaven or must first undergo a period of punishment before ultimately being restored to God's good graces. Hosea Ballou was a proponent of the first position, his distant relative Adin Ballou an advocate of the eventually triumphant second. Some modern historians have even suggested that the only reason the Restorationist Controversy is remembered at all is because Hosea Ballou's early biographer, Thomas Whittemore, made it seem important; it was the one anomalous episode in which his subject (and mentor) had been on the "losing" side of an issue, and as such, had to be explained.

THEOLOGICAL CONTROVERSY, INSTITUTIONAL CONFLICT, AND HISTORICAL CONSCIOUSNESS

In many ways, the organizational challenges confronting Unitarians and Universalists as they attempted to transform themselves from theological movements into effective denominational institutions were exactly opposite. The Universalists spent much of the early nineteenth century scrambling to catch up to the wave of popular growth that at first accompanied their movement, and then later struggled to keep afloat numerous marginal concerns with minimal resources. Unitarians, on the other hand, enjoyed an embarrassment of riches, but were reluctant to move out of their comfortable environment into the wilderness beyond "the neighborhood of Boston." In both cases, the controversies turned out to be more vocal than substantive, and ultimately more distracting than divisive. Finally, both the Unitarians and the Universalists looked to history in order to articulate a core identity around which both a theological consensus and effective structures for denominational cooperation might coalesce.

For example, Hosea Ballou 2d sought to ground Universalist doctrine in early church practice in his *Ancient History of Universalism*. In the writings of third-century church father Origen, he identified vestiges of the doctrine of universal salvation, representative of an early Christianity that had its strongest influence among the marginalized lower classes of the Roman empire. Together with a companion volume by Thomas Whittemore, *Modern History of Universalism*, this sort of scholarly polemic represented the desire on the part of Universalists to see themselves as part of a larger, continuous historical tradition, and therefore as respectable members of the mainstream Christian community.

Unlike their Universalist country cousins, Unitarians had little need to legitimize their movement through an appeal to history. From an institutional perspective, Unitarians were for all practical purposes the official church establishment in eastern Massachusetts by 1825. This position of privilege gave them a legitimacy grounded in the legacy of the Pilgrim Fathers themselves. But even privilege is not without its drawbacks. Thus, while the Universalists found themselves facing the challenge of legitimizing their distinctive theology through an appeal to history, the Unitarians looked to the past to resolve an identity crisis. Where is the theological center of a community defined principally by its latitude?

Demographically, nineteenth-century Unitarians were highly homogeneous. Denominational identity derived as much from the shared network of social, educational, and family relationships as from any sense of common ideology or mission. And like the Victorian society in which they lived, they approached the world with a confident air of privileged superiority that at times reeked of arrogance. For example, nineteenth-century Unitarians were justly proud of their lack of dogmatism and of their early attempts at social ministry among the poor Irish immigrants of Boston and New York. It seems clear in retrospect, however, that this deeply-felt sense of noblesse oblige was rooted more in a belief that the "enlightened" values of rational religious discourse, together with the "self-culture" of individual character, would ultimately displace the "superstitious ritualism" of Roman Catholicism than it was in any notion of religious toleration or respect for diversity of belief.

Within this demographic homogeneity of privilege, theological controversy plagued nineteenth-century Unitarians. The Transcendentalist Controversy involved far more than possibly can be discussed here, but it is essential to acknowledge that, for better or worse, Transcendentalism shaped Unitarian self-understanding so pervasively in the nineteenth century that today it is difficult not to see its vestiges wherever one looks. The Transcendentalists' philosophical idealism and nature-based mysticism provided fresh emphasis on the authority of personal religious experience as a source of religious truth, while their interest in societal and institutional reform inspired not only communitarian utopian experiments such as Brook Farm and Fruitlands, but also innovative new congregations organized according to the so-called "voluntary principle," such as Theodore Parker's 28th Congregational Society and James Freeman Clarke's Church of the Disciples. Even those for whom "Parkerism" represented nothing more than "the latest form of infidelity" found themselves drawn into the melodrama by the radicals, who sought to cast them in the same role that the "orthodox" had played a generation before.

Theodore Parker's 1843 "heresy trial" before the Boston Association of Ministers became a kind of sine qua non for framing the controversy. A de facto Unitarian organization, the association was a long-standing fraternal order of area clergy who regularly exchanged pulpits and who spoke in rotation at the "Great and Thursday Lecture" at Boston's First Church. Pastor of a small suburban parish in West Roxbury, Theodore Parker was admitted to the group in 1837, but as he grew more outspoken about his theological views, members grew wary. In an emotionally charged confrontation, Parker refused to resign his membership and the members declined in turn to throw him out, citing their confidence in the quality of his character even as they distanced themselves from the content of this theology.

In 1873 William James Potter intentionally evoked the spirit of Parker in sparking the so-called Yearbook Controversy. Potter was secretary of the Free Religious Association, a small group of theological radicals organized in 1867 in reaction to the adoption of the phrase "the Lord Jesus Christ" in the preamble of the Constitution of the first National Conference of Unitarian Churches two years earlier. An exchange of letters between Potter and AUA secretary George Fox resulted in Potter's name being dropped from the 1874 list of Unitarian ministers, ostensibly on the grounds that Potter no longer considered himself a Christian. The resulting controversy engendered a public scandal around perceived issues of denominational intolerance. It added fire to the argument over whether even something so simple as a "Statement of Things Commonly Believed Among Us To-Day," while not a creed, qualified as a creedlet. The question was whether Unitarians must believe alike in order to work together, or if it was enough simply to agree to cooperate and to remain in conversation with all people of goodwill and a liberal spirit.

This last sentiment, the cry of wide-ranging tolerance, became the central tenet of the institution builders, "broad church" Unitarians such as Henry Whitney Bellows, Frederic Henry Hedge, and James Freeman Clarke. Clarke's famous statement, "The Fatherhood of God, The Brotherhood of Man, The Leadership of Jesus, Salvation by Character, and the Progress of Mankind onward and upward forever," is not only an excellent summary of late nineteenth-century Unitarian belief, but it also refutes the five points of traditional Calvinism by invoking many of the ideas popular among the radicals. God's sovereignty is affirmed, but his nature is that of a loving parent/stern disciplinarian, not an omnipotent monarch and judge. Christ's example and leadership are important, not any vicarious atoning sacrifice. The themes of a common human family, self-culture, and evolutionary progress are all emphasized.

William Channing Gannett's hymn, "It Sounds Along the Ages," similarly reflects a notion of absolute religion. Moses, the Buddha, Socrates, and Christ all "one holy word declare." An "eternal chime" echoed in "the hammer stroke of Luther," "the Pilgrim's seaside prayer," and Ralph Waldo Emerson's "oracles of Concord." Essentially prophetic in nature, this timeless call of soul to soul represents a spirit of truth and justice that human institutions can only imperfectly embody. A basic consensus regarding Unitarian identity eventually formed around this understanding of the relationship of theology to history.

Although it is tempting to describe the various controversies between nineteenth-century religious liberals in theological terms, the conflict is more accurately characterized as between those whose understanding of the basis of religious fellowship tended to be *ideo-*

logically oriented and those whose orientation was more *institutional-ly focused*. The ideologues were strongly opposed to any kind of explicit statement of theological belief, while the institutionalists typically felt that such statements were organizationally useful, although the specific content was always open to discussion. This tension, never fully resolved, did diminish as the nineteenth century came to a close due to new consensus regarding the historical parameters of liberal religious identity.

Several factors contributed to create a broader cultural and intellectual context for turn-of-the-century Unitarianism and Universalism: the shifting relationship between science and religion following the development of evolutionary theory; the dramatic social changes brought about by industrial urban capitalism; new familiarity with non-Western religions; and changing paradigms of Biblical criticism, and even of historical scholarship itself. To articulate their religious message in an increasingly secular, liberalized society, religious liberals adopted themes of the social gospel and a new emphasis on rationalism and the "religion of humanity," and attempted to identify the "Universal Unity" that undergirds all authentic religious faith. The ecumenical social activism of Universalist Clarence Skinner and Unitarian John Haynes Holmes found expression in the Community Church movement, which essentially sought to transform religious congregations into nonsectarian agencies for transforming society itself. Likewise, the publication of the "Humanist Manifesto" in the early 1930s continued to push the sectarian boundaries of denominational inclusiveness, while at the same time drawing Unitarianism and Universalism more tightly into one another's orbit.

Yet even as Unitarianism in particular broadened the parameters of its fellowship, it also looked within and to its past to determine its religious center. A key figure was Earl Morse Wilbur, whose work brought American Unitarians to a new level of historical consciousness. Wilbur's 1925 book, *Our Unitarian Heritage,* was followed twenty years later by his monumental two-volume work, *A History of Unitarianism,* the culmination of his unprecedented scholarly inquiry into the nature and scope of anti-trinitarian thought from the time of Servetus to the twentieth century. It was Wilbur who characterized the essence of Unitarianism as a belief in freedom, reason, and tolerance, not as "the final goals to be aimed at in religion" but rather "conditions under which the true ends may best be attained."

MYTHOS AND MERGER

The eventual merger of the Unitarians and the Universalists may seem obvious in retrospect, but it was anything but inevitable. Many Universalists were hesitant about the prospect, wary that their identity would be subsumed within the larger Unitarian movement and also cautious about Unitarianism's reputation for radicalism and the absence of a strong Christian identity. If merger were to happen, a new set of identity questions needed resolution.

Much of the success of merger can be attributed to the two denominations having taken the time to do the groundwork beforehand. The process began with the formation of the Free Church Fellowship in the 1930s and included numerous cooperative ventures prior to actual merger, including the development of shared youth organizations and a common Service Committee. Rigorous self-scrutiny and interdenominational dialogue helped focus the issues of uniting the two fellowships, while the leadership of Frederick May Eliot and Dana McLean Greeley for the Unitarians and Brainard Gibbons and Philip Randall Giles for the Universalists, all of whom favored "consolidation," was likewise very influential. On the larger cultural scene the influence of the postwar ecumenical movement exerted a powerful impetus to closer cooperation throughout all Christendom. Although Universalist fears that the consolidation of resources would strike hardest at its traditional seminaries and other institutions proved well founded, the ultimate success of merger can be seen in its widespread acceptance on the local congregational level.

In articulating their new merged identity, Unitarian Universalists emphasized both denominations' bias for practical morality and heritage of progressive social action. Hierarchy was rejected in favor of democracy and a belief in the value of human solidarity. The ideal of an evolving universal religion stood side by side with the notion of a "pure" Christianity unsullied by sectarian dogma, as well as the implicit recognition of the value of rationalism, a positive view of science and historical Biblical criticism, and of course, the traditional doctrines of universal salvation and anti-trinitarianism that had originally distinguished the two movements. Central to all was the understanding that Unitarian Universalism would be without a creed, a non-confessional faith that acted on its beliefs rather than merely repeating them on Sunday mornings.

The relationship between the institutional and the ideological aspects of Unitarian Universalism remains an important focus for denominational self-understanding. In the 1990s, for example, Americans identified themselves as "Unitarian" to pollsters at levels three to ten times higher than are reflected in the membership lists of Unitarian Universalist congregations. Theological positions that at one time would have distinguished Unitarians and Universalists from other faiths are now commonplace throughout the mainline denominations. The Free Religionists of the nineteenth century had dismissed the "peculiar" elements that distinguished the "historical" religions from one another as corruptions of the "Universal Unity" that was the source of all authentic religious belief. Ironically, on the threshold of the third millennium, Unitarian Universalists find themselves concerned not only with what they have in common with the other religious faiths of the world, but also with whether any special theological or institutional characteristics make Unitarian-Universalism unique.

At the 1984 and 1985 General Assemblies, the Unitarian Universalist Association adopted a new preamble to its bylaws that identified seven Principles and five "Sources of the Living Tradition We Share." The division of the statement into these two categories—one focused on ideology and the other on heritage—is itself indicative of the important role historical tradition continues to play in determining Unitarian Universalist identity. The subsequent decision to organize the new hymnal, *Singing the Living Tradition,* around categories that reflect these historical sources reinforces this sense that Unitarian Universalists continue to seek their future through an appreciation of their past. In 1995 a sixth source, the "Spiritual Teachings of Earth-Centered Traditions," was amended to the list of sources. While some felt this move was wrong-headed, given the movement's historical propensity to bicker about "creeping creedalism," the General Assembly's decision to identify a new source rather than articulate a new principle is itself indicative of the role tradition plays in legitimizing segments of an increasingly eclectic ideological community.

At the same time, this renewed historical interest in heritage and tradition has expressed itself in the worship life of Unitarian Universalism. An emerging concern with ritual and spirituality reflects a yearning on the part of many individual Unitarian

Universalists to ground themselves in a sense of the ultimate through repetition of activities that embody traditional significance. The widespread use of the flaming chalice is one example of how a symbol representing a particular period of history in which Unitarian and Universalist values were dramatically evidenced has been incorporated into the devotional practice of an ongoing community of faith.

Marion Franklin Ham's 1933 hymn, "Our Kindred Fellowships" (identified in the current hymnal by its first line, "As Tranquil Streams"), reflects this process as well. Originally composed to celebrate the growing cooperation between Unitarians and Universalists, the lyrics compare the merging of the two traditions to the meeting of two rivers that "flow as one to meet the sea." Freedom from "narrow thought and lifeless creed" as well as from the hypocrisy of "a social code that fails to serve the cause of human need" are the qualities defining its "liberating ministry." Yet it is also a "Freedom that reveres the past, but trusts the dawning future more; and bids the soul in search of truth, adventure boldly and explore." Armed with "the power of love," this "prophetic church" proclaims "the truth that makes us free," echoing not only the words of John's Gospel but the promise of an evolving, universal religion. In its most recent casting, however, the words "our kindred fellowships" have been replaced by "our kindred hearts and minds." The change, though subtle, is significant. What were once two distinct fellowships, each with unique historical identity and traditions, have been internalized in the lives of worshipping individuals.

It has sometimes been said that nostalgia is the dead hand of the living, but tradition is the living hand of the dead. If we look to our past solely through the misty eyes of sentimentalism, we will see there only a superficial reflection of ourselves. But when we allow our spiritual forebears to speak to us authentically in their own voices, we will discover in their experience potential mentors for our own religious pilgrimage. The great truths of religion are eternal. Yet in every generation each individual must discover and embrace those truths in his or her own way if they are to evoke the power to transform a person's life. This is the miracle of a "living tradition"—the ability to create anew the wisdom of "words made flesh," and to reveal in the lives of those who have come before us the insights that can guide us as we encounter our own future.

Questions for Discussion

1. Tim W. Jensen outlines the separate histories of the American Unitarian and Universalist movements and notes that "Unitarian Universalism" is a construct created, in part, from these histories. To what extent does this construct incorporate these traditions, and to what extent is today's Unitarian Universalism something new? Do we adequately celebrate our histories?

2. Jensen contrasts ideological and institutional thrusts seen in the history of both movements. Examples include liberal Christians and Transcendentalists, ultra-universalists and restorationists, free religionists and "broad church" Unitarians. Can you debate the two viewpoints in each? Is this same tension seen in our congregations today? In the UUA?

3. Jensen sees evidence of Unitarian Universalists today seeking to connect with a historical tradition and religious practices in various ways, for example, rituals such as chalice lighting, spiritual practices such as meditation, emphasis on sources underlying our stated principles. Do you agree? Do you see other examples of this trend? What is its significance?

The Wise Weakness of the
Congregational Way

Earl K. Holt III

Editor's Note. Earl Holt provides a lucid explanation of congregational polity. He reviews the evolution of our form of church governance and illuminates its historical significance. He then concludes with a discussion of the contemporary free church movement in the context of our movement-wide efforts to institutionalize freedom effectively. Holt is a graduate of Brown University and Starr King School for the Ministry. He has served as minister of First Unitarian Church of St. Louis since 1974. He is the author of William Greenleaf Eliot, Conservative Radical *and numerous articles of church history and congregational polity. This essay was originally presented at the 1997 Conference on the Free Church in Tulsa, and subsequently part of it appeared in the* UU Voice. *It is published here in slightly revised form by permission of the author.*

Our churches belong to the Unitarian Universalist Association (UUA). We loosely refer to "the denomination," but strictly speaking, an association is not a denomination. The UUA is made up of about a thousand independent and autonomous congregations joined in a voluntary association. The relationship of the congregations to the association is precisely parallel to the relationship of individual members to their congregations. We join voluntarily, we support our congregations and work voluntarily, and we may withdraw at will. The association has no ecclesiastical, theological, political, or any other authority over its member congregations. In the language of the UUA Bylaws, it is "a voluntary association of autonomous, self-governing local churches and fellowships . . . which have freely chosen to pursue common goals together."

This form of church governance is known as congregational polity. In terms of the distinctiveness of our way of religion, congregational polity is at least as important as the noncreedal principle, if not more so. A "church" in this tradition and by this understanding is one thing and one thing only: an individual congregation whose primary covenant is to and among its own members. In this tradition there are no bishops by any name, no synod, presbytery, episcopate; no organized body or individual outside the congregation may dictate or direct the decisions and activities that go on within it. The individual church owns its own properties, elects its own ministers and other church officers, and conducts all its own affairs. I refer to this structure, even more than to our devotion to the principle of individual freedom of belief, when I say that ours is a free church. This structure of organization is otherwise known as the congregational way.

The first legal name of our church in St. Louis, gathered in 1835, was the First Congregational Church, referring not to a theological stance or a denominational connection, but to its form of organization. The St. Louis church was organized with financial and other support from the American Unitarian Association, at that time little more than a clergyman's club organized in Boston a decade earlier. That association was from its beginning characterized by a fierce devotion to the congregational way. In fact, the great founding father of Unitarianism in this country, William Ellery Channing, declined election as the first president of the Unitarian Association in 1825 expressly because he feared any tendency toward denominationalism and away from congregational independence. I understand Channing. In my observation the natural, normal, and indeed almost irresistible tendency of all human organization is toward centralization, hierarchy, systemization, and authoritarianism. To avoid these tendencies is to practice that "eternal vigilance" that Thomas Jefferson said was the price of liberty.

You don't have to look far or very hard to find abundant illustrations of the powerful centripetal tendencies working against congregational freedom. Even before their merger into the United Church of Christ (UCC) thirty years ago, the more traditional Congregational churches had begun the move away from ecclesiastical independence, vesting the power of ordination of ministers in church councils, for example. The spirit of true congregationalism lives on, not in the UCC, but in the more than 400 churches across the country that stayed out of the merger, reaffirmed their commitment to congregational autonomy, and organized themselves separately into a truly voluntary association, the National Association of Congregational Christian Churches. (Those 431 Congregational churches, by the way, have a total membership not a lot smaller than the 150,000 or so adult members we have in our Unitarian Universalist churches. They are served by a national professional staff of four, with expenses considerably lower than those of the UUA, whose current annual operating budget is something in excess of $10 million.) At first by accident and then by design, our Midwest district minister's group has met with these independent Congregational ministers at a retreat center near Chicago. These meetings have informed and strengthened my sense of the importance of maintaining the congregational way.

So, just exactly what is the congregational way? A couple of years ago I offered an answer to this question to my congregation in the form of three short articles I called a "Crash Course on Congregational Polity," which went something like this.

CRASH COURSE IN CONGREGATIONAL POLITY

Technically, we are not a denomination, though we call ourselves one anyway. We refer to the denomination as "continental," not "national," in recognition of our Canadian congregations.

In the Constitution and Bylaws of the UUA, the congregational nature of our association was and is explicitly affirmed. "The [UUA] is a voluntary association of autonomous, self-governing local churches and fellowships . . . which have freely chosen to pursue common goals together." Congregational polity and individual freedom of belief were the two definitive principles of the Unitarians. Proponents of national organization always struggle against centrifugal forces, though, paradoxical as it may seem, the Unitarians produced some strong national presidents and gave them real authority in a time, admittedly very different from our own, when such "patriarchal" leadership was still possible.

As the Universalists declined in numbers, the most talented of their leaders focused their energy and interests increasingly in the arena of the national church. Presbyterian (hierarchical form of church governance) rather than congregational in their historic structure, the Universalist leadership by 1961 consisted of a highly unified group of mostly ministers who constituted something like a de facto national board of elders (though in fact most of them were quite young) who shared much in common theologically with the more humanistically inclined among the Unitarians. (When we speak these days, as many do, of reclaiming our Universalist heritage, it is crucial to understand that we are not talking about late Universalist forms of organization. That is my point here.)

When the Unitarians and Universalists united in 1961, they adopted the Unitarian structures then in place. Of particular importance was the affirmation of radical congregational polity central to the Unitarian tradition. This may have been a principled decision, but it was also convenient in a tactical or political sense, for it meant the national reorganization would in theory have no effect on the life of local congregations of either denomination. One result was that no significant or organized body of churches refused to unite with the new association, as in the UCC merger.

Purists insist that what is commonly called "merger" was and should be referred to as "consolidation." By either name what is referred to is the 1961 joining of two groups that had been carrying on a decades-long affair, the American Unitarian Association and the Universalist Church of America. At the time the Unitarians were vigorous and growing, the Universalists small and declining. Note that the Unitarians were an "association" and the Universalists a "church." The difference is not insignificant. I believe that a struggle has been going on ever since over whether we understand our movement still to be an association of autonomous congregations (what we say on paper) or more of a unified church (increasingly how we behave).

In practical terms we have been struggling for more than three decades now, for the most part unconsciously, with these two differing understandings of "church" represented by the two different traditions. Many of the strongest and most talented leaders among the Universalists had for a long time been the primary activists in their national church. A disproportionate number of them came to occupy positions of importance and influence in the new Unitarian Universalist Association. Although to date all the UUA presidents have been nurtured in the Unitarian tradition, many major offices from the executive vice president through department heads were held by Universalists, especially in the formative years.

I need to say that obviously my summary here is an oversimplification. History does not lend itself to neat categories or patterns.

Besides, there have been by now two generations of "UUs" who do not relate particularly to the name of either historic tradition.

But I do believe that over the twenty-five years I have served in our ministry, there has been an observable decline in understanding and appreciation of the congregational way, radical congregational polity, and individual freedom of belief. In the ascendent is what's technically named sectarianism (referring to a larger religious body breaking up into smaller groups, each with its own special requirements and beliefs) and a sect called Unitarian Universalism. The centrifugal tendencies of the congregational way are in tension with the centripetal forces of the sect. The direction is away from a self-understanding of our movement as an association of independent congregations and toward a denominational church with local subsidiaries, or "franchises." It is symbolized most dramatically in the trend toward renaming historic churches according to the brand label of the denomination.

But the shift in power relations in our association is more than symbolic. The loss of the sense of congregational autonomy and the increased dependence of churches on denominational bureaucracy and structures in critical dimensions of their lives should be of great concern to all. Yet those concerns have been addressed for the most part in such forums as late night grumble sessions at ministers' gatherings. The convening of the 1997 Tulsa Conference on the Free Church gave many ministers a chance to address the issues more formally and directly. I think before we abandon congregational polity willy-nilly, we certainly ought to understand what we are in danger of losing.

In the course of preparing this paper I have carefully reviewed the UUA Bylaws. The phrase "congregational polity" is used several times, but without precision.

Congregational polity is about the relations between and among individual congregations. It derives from Puritan/Congregational understandings of the church codified in great detail in a document called the Cambridge Platform, adopted by a church council in New England in 1648. Before any of our churches were called Unitarian, they were called Congregational, this name referring not to a denomination or a theology but to their polity, or form of governance.

In the same loose and inaccurate way in which it is sometimes said that "being Unitarian means you can believe whatever you want," it is sometimes said that congregational polity means that "a congregation can do whatever it wants." There is just enough truth in either statement to make confusion easy and clarity all the more important. Congregational polity is not about the independence of individual churches but about the *right relationship* of independent churches. Or as Conrad Wright, the most important scholar in the field, has put it many times, congregational polity means "not the autonomy of the local church, but the community of autonomous churches." As we understand each of our congregations as a body of individuals united in a covenantal community, so should we explicitly understand our association as a covenantal community of congregations.

Being in covenantal community is no easier for independent-minded churches than it is for independent-minded individuals. Seeking to avoid the hierarchy and authoritarianism of the Church of England and for theological reasons, too, the Puritans vested ecclesiastical authority solely in the local church. How then would they settle issues of conflict, discipline, and order? Mainly, they said, by consultation with other like-minded bodies. Inter-church relations in congregational churches are lateral, neighborly, consultative. Decisions are the result of persuasion and reasoned discussion, not coercion or assignment of authority to bishops or boards of elders. The community of churches is built by friendly relations. Collegiality is a key word, referring not just to relations among clergy but between and among congregations. Conferences and councils, called into session to deal with inter- and intra-church conflicts and controversies as well as other matters of general importance, were a regular feature of congregational church order and discipline. Ordaining councils, with participation of clergy and lay leaders from several churches, were perhaps the most common example. The authority of such councils, called upon to address all manner of contested matters, was inevitably in tension with the prerogatives granted by congregational independence, but generally their advice was heeded and always respected. It is, I believe, the system most likely to promote and preserve freedom, reason, and tolerance among those who share an understanding of its practice, and it is a system I believe we can and ought to reclaim and renew.

A couple of years ago I participated in a panel at General Assembly, sponsored by our Commission on Appraisal, addressing the subject, Is congregational polity necessary to Unitarian

Universalism? My answer was, and is, maybe not, but it is, I believe, necessary to the free church, the truly liberal church. It is necessary because liberalism is not a doctrine, not a creed, not a list of purposes and principles. It is a spirit and process, a way of being. And its primary goal, its real purpose, is to protect freedom of individual conscience and the right of dissent in community, in institutions.

Institutionalists such as myself appreciate the value of loyalty. I have tried throughout my ministry to encourage loyalty to the association of which our church in St. Louis, like yours, is a part. But my larger loyalty is to the heritage of the free church, and key to that is the congregational polity that has protected its freedom.

THE PARADOX OF INSTITUTIONALIZING FREEDOM

There is, of course, a paradoxical element in all of this. It arises because what we are about as a religious movement is institutionalizing religious freedom, and freedom is not easy to institutionalize. We know this from the experience of our American history, which is the history of the attempt to institutionalize freedom in political terms. And we know it from our own history and present experience as a religious movement.

As I see it, there are presently two competing tendencies within our association, one affirming the primacy of congregational polity and the free church tradition. The other, visibly gaining ground, is moving steadily, if unconsciously, in the direction of making us less a diversified movement and more a unified church in the ordinary understanding of that word, a church called Unitarian Universalist.

I overstate, for the sake of emphasis, the fact that our historical movement has always put individual liberty of conscience at the head of its defining principles. The emerging church has increasingly used the Purposes and Principles statement adopted some years ago at our General Assembly as at least a quasi creed, not just as a symbol of unity underlying our diversity, but as a proof-text for defining an ideology called Unitarian Universalism. It is, one might note, emblazoned on the opening pages of the new UUA hymnal, right where the Episcopalians and the Presbyterians print the Apostle's Creed.

Institutionally, our historical movement has always understood itself to be an association of free and autonomous congregations organized from the bottom up in voluntary cooperation on areas of common interest. Institutionally, the emerging church is tending toward becoming a corporate entity with ultimate responsibility for all matters of church discipline centralized in the offices of the staff and board.

Ecclesiastically, our historical movement was radically congregational, with each congregation conscious of its unique power and the responsibilities of that power, especially in the calling and ordaining of our ministers. The emerging church moves increasingly in the direction I jokingly on previous occasions, and now seriously, refer to as "creeping Methodism." It has obscured the distinction between its credentialing power, the granting of Fellowship, and that of ordination, the exclusive province of individual congregations. It has evolved an appointment system for many new ministers and ministries as well as interim ministries. There has even been a casual suggestion to adopt non-congregational ordination.

Technically, our wider movement is drifting in the direction of sectarianism. It is a tendency natural to all religious movements and one William Ellery Channing warned against at the very beginning of our American history.

I would like new members of our churches to understand that in joining this church they are not allying themselves with a bureaucracy in Boston called the Unitarian Universalist Association. They are not joining a sect called Unitarian Universalism. They are not even becoming Unitarian Universalists. Rather, they are allying themselves with something much larger and much more important than anything categorized under a denominational label or religious brand name. They are connecting themselves with the great and noble heritage of the free faith. They are connecting themselves to the great and good of every generation that has stood against all idolatries and hindrances to the spirit, to those who have stood for truth as they saw it, even at the ultimate cost to themselves. They are connecting themselves with the freedom fighters and freedom lovers of every age and every race and nationality and every religion.

If that all sounds rather cosmic, let me conclude with something more basic and intimate. I believe that the success of our way of faith, of our religious movement, has derived from the priority it has given to the individual congregation, remarkable assemblages every one, face-to-face, relatively intimate human communities where we know each other by name, where our faith is both nurtured and challenged in close connection and communion with other seekers and searchers. When I think of who we are as a religious people, I do not think of a creed or a quasi creed, Purposes and Principles, words on a plaque. I do not think of the headquarters building in Boston, impressive as it is. I do not think of our UUA president, good friend and fine man that he is, as good a man as has ever held that office. Rather, I think of congregations I have preached to all across the land and their places of worship, each with a unique history and as different from one another as the individuals who gather there.

A Free Church for a Free People

Our polity is not incidental to our identity; what we are institutionally is part of who we are religiously. Yet newcomers are not likely to think much about the matters we are discussing today. It used to be said that the only thing Unitarians could agree on were Robert's Rules of Order and congregational polity. Yet in many of our churches today relatively few members have much understanding of the nature, let alone the significance, of our polity.

Nor is this surprising when you think about it, which I hadn't until recently. Here is something so obvious that I couldn't believe it had not occurred to me before. Well over 90 percent of the members of our churches have become Unitarian Universalists in their own lifetimes. The vast majority of these people come either from no particular church background or from churches very different from our own, different not just in theology but in ecclesiology. And while we have laid much stress in our education materials on the theological distinctiveness of our movement, we have done almost nothing to educate either our children or our adults on the history or significance of our polity. So it is no surprise really that many of our lay people are profoundly ignorant about this element of our tradition and as a result often quite amenable to proposals that violate congregational principles.

Among the most significant of these violations have been what I gently call the "over-functioning" of the association's fellowship committee, the committee charged with reviewing the qualifications of those seeking settlement in our churches, and the inattention to congregational integrity in the virtual appointment of ministers to so-called extension churches within our movement. I have written extensively about these and a variety of related issues over the

years, but it has occurred to me to wonder why it has been necessary. For a long time I attributed it to the observable tendency
toward centralization of authority and power in all organizations.
But fueling it as well, I believe, is the suspicion that our weakness as
a religious movement is attributable to our congregationalism. We
are, it is felt, so damnably independent. If only we could organize
ourselves more efficiently. If only we could adopt definite standards
for our ministers and enforce them in an ongoing way. If only we
didn't have to let the churches decide what is good for them in terms
of leadership. And on and on. The bottom line of this line of thinking, though it is really more a feeling than an argument, is that somehow our relative puniness in numbers is an organizational problem,
that congregational polity begets small churches and political inef-
fectiveness.

Two observations: First, consider the opposite extreme, a cookie-
cutter, franchise approach to religion. It does work. Look at the
Mormons. Last summer my brother Rick, an architect in New
Hampshire, pointed out to me two brand new Mormon churches in
small towns in that state, some miles apart. They used the same
building plan for both, just as McDonald's does—efficient, coherent,
systematic—and spiritually deadly. Such an approach is unimagin-
able in a church that professes belief in individual integrity and personal accountability. Second, look at the Baptists. Perhaps farthest
from us theologically, the Southern Baptists are our closest cousins
in ecclesiology. They are by some millions the largest Protestant
denomination in the country. Again, I use the term *denomination*
loosely; in fact, every Baptist church is an independent entity and
preciously guards its autonomy. Although in recent years their
national convention has been taken over by extremely conservative
fundamentalists, individual churches have been free to go their own
quite different ways—until just recently, that is, when for the first
time the national convention voted to eject two congregations, one
that had ordained a homosexual as its minister, the other that had
given spiritual sanction to a homosexual union.

THE WISE WEAKNESS
OF THE CONGREGATIONAL WAY

More than twenty years ago I heard a former president of our association, Bob West, use an analogy framed by a Revolutionary soldier

named Ames, who compared monarchy to a great sailing ship, large and stately and magnificent on the high seas, which, however, was threatened by storms and shallows in which it could easily founder and sink. "Democracy," Ames said, "is more like a raft, virtually unsinkable, but your feet are always wet." The congregational way is like democracy in this respect. As Churchill said, it is the worst form of government except for all the others. It can be frustrating in its weakness, its inefficiency, and your feet are always wet, but it is virtually unsinkable. Would that we would all work, then, not for more bureaucratic efficiency, but for more wet feet in our community of free congregations!

The Puritans—from whom we have inherited this tradition of congregational polity—spoke of the congregation as the Body of Christ. Most of us would choose different words, but we would mean what they meant, which is that whatever wholeness, holiness, or hope there is resides in us and among us, with us in a particular religious community, a congregation. This is the bright and bold promise of the congregational way. I pray that we may be conscious of the preciousness and importance of this heritage, and that we may serve it well.

Questions for Discussion

1. Earl K. Holt affirms, "Congregational polity is not about the independence of individual congregations but about the *right relationship* of independent churches," and cites Conrad Wright's term, "the community of autonomous churches." He describes a system of lateral relationships among congregations, predating the emergence of denominational structures in the last century, and suggests renewing these informal or ad hoc ways of being in "right relationship." What are the practical implications of this proposal? What is the problem it would ease or solve?

2. Holt defines liberalism as "a spirit and a process, a way of being," the "real purpose" of which "is to protect freedom of individual conscience and the right of dissent in community, in institutions." Do you agree that "liberalism" is primarily a negative principle, protecting individual freedom vis-á-vis the community or society, or that it is primarily a positive principle, expressing confidence in the human capacity to act freely for the common good?

3. Holt is concerned that criticism of congregational polity as a principle of independence and individual freedom is rooted in concern for denominational growth. He also feels that its true meaning is not understood because more than 90 percent of Unitarian Universalists have come from other religious backgrounds; thus, we violate our free church heritage by treating the Principles of the UUA like a creed. Do you agree?

4. Consider that 90 percent of Unitarian Universalists coming from other religious backgrounds signifies the failure of a 200-year-old religious movement to retain its own children, and that the congregations in the UUA today claim approximately the same number of members as at the time of merger in 1961. Do you think that devotion to "the wise weakness of the congregational way" is the cure or the problem?

Congregational Polity and the Covenant

Conrad Wright

Editor's Note. In the following essay, Conrad Wright reviews the historical role of the covenant in congregational polity. He concludes that the free church needs the sense of mutual obligation and commitment it provides. Wright is perhaps the most respected living scholar of liberal religion. He is professor emeritus of American church history at Harvard Divinity School and the author of countless authoritative papers and books, including the recently published Congregational Polity *(Skinner House Books, 1997). He received the UUA Distinguished Service Award in 1988.*

The polity of Unitarian Universalist churches is congregational, rather than presbyterian or episcopal (these are the two most common forms of hierarchical church government). To be sure, there can be considerable variation in actual practice among churches adhering to congregational polity. Unitarian Universalists like to think of themselves as more properly congregational than the Congregationalists, now part of the United Church of Christ, who have accepted some elements of presbyterian hierarchical control. On the other hand, many conservative churches reject any denominational organization comparable to the Unitarian Universalist Association (UUA) as much too centralized, as well as quite unscriptural. The essential principle of congregational polity, however, is found when ultimate authority rests in the local society.

Our way of practicing congregational polity goes back to the great Puritan migration to New England in the 1630s. Some of our older churches were gathered at that time and have been self-governing ever since. The Puritans set forth the principles of their polity in *A Platform of Church Discipline* (1648), commonly referred to as the Cambridge Platform. It carefully defines both the "matter" of the

visible church, that is, the qualifications of those who are the material of which the church is composed, and the "form" of the visible
church, that is, what it is that transforms a collection of religiously
concerned individuals into a religious community. The language of
the Puritans is not ours, and some parts of their definitions have been
discarded in the course of generations, but certain basic essentials are
to be found there that are as important today as they were then.

The "matter" of the visible church was defined in the Platform as
"saints by calling"—those who, there is good reason to believe, will
be numbered among the righteous at the Day of Judgment. We no
longer believe in the Day of Judgment, at least in that sense, nor do
we accept the Calvinistic doctrine of election. But we still would
agree that full church membership involving both privileges and
obligations depends on a conscious, voluntary decision. Our children may be born with the watch and care of a religious community, and we may acknowledge that fact by a ceremony of baptism,
christening, or consecration, but it is only when they approach
adulthood and are made aware of the significance of the act that
they may decide to seek membership.

Adopting the typology made familiar by Ernst Troeltsch, we may
say that congregationalism is the polity of religious groups of the
sect type, as contrasted with the church type. For Troeltsch, the
church is that form of religious organization that seeks to be coex-
tensive with a whole society. A national church, like the Church of
England in the early seventeenth century, would be the example
most closely conforming to the ideal type. All inhabitants of the
realm were presumptively part of the established church. Those
who lived in a particular parish were part of that parish by birth and
domicile, not by their own choice. The sect, on the other hand, is
formed by the voluntary association of like-minded believers. Thus
the Puritans, who protested what they saw as corruption in the
established church, sought one another out for mutual aid and com-
fort and found the true church in small communities of faithful
souls. The sect was their type of organization; congregationalism or
"independence" was their polity.

For a community of the faithful to come into being, however,
propinquity is not enough. "Saints by calling" says the Cambridge
Platform, "must have a Visible-Political-Union amongst themselves,
or else they are not yet a particular church." There must be some
organizational basis, or form, so that individual believers may be

orderly knit together. This form is the visible covenant, or agreement, commonly called the church covenant. From the church as a community, one is entitled to expect care and concern for one's own well-being, but one is equally obligated to express care and concern for others. Therefore, an element of commitment exists in the act of joining a church, which the covenant expresses.

The authors of the Cambridge Platform acknowledged that a covenant might be implicit, expressed by silent consent as people walk together and show concern for one another. But an explicit covenant is far better, they argued, for reminding the members of their mutual duty and stirring them up to it. When a church was gathered, therefore, the covenant would be read and all would give their assent to it. When the church exercised discipline over its members, offenses would be understood as breaches of the covenant. If a member removed to some other community, he or she did not silently disappear but sought dismissal and release from the obligations of the covenant.

The earliest New England covenants were simple statements of agreement to walk together. The Salem Covenant of 1629 is only one sentence long: "We Covenant with the Lord and one with another; and doe bynd ourselves in the presence of God, to walke together in all his waies, according as he is pleased to reveale himself unto us in his Blessed word of truth." The Boston Covenant of 1630 is slightly longer but expresses the same intention: "to walke in all our wayes according to the Rule of the Gospell, and in all sincere Conformity to His holy Ordinaunces, and in mutual love, and respect each to other, so neere as God shall give us grace."

These early covenants did not take the form of creedal statements, nor did they prescribe doctrinal standards for admission to church fellowship. That is not because diversity of doctrinal belief was acceptable, but because theological uniformity could be taken for granted and did not need to be spelled out. But uniformity of belief cannot be maintained indefinitely, and later on the simple covenants were rewritten to include creedal formulations. In the eighteenth century, when religious liberalism began to appear and Arminian and anti-trinitarian views found expression in some quarters, the orthodox fenced in their churches with very explicit creedal covenants.

The covenant gave form to the particular church, but the church was not the only ecclesiastical body in early New England. Until the demise of the Standing Order (Connecticut in 1818, New Hampshire in 1819, Massachusetts in 1833), it was the town, or the parish as a subdivision of a town, that was obligated to support the public worship of God. All inhabitants, not just church members, were liable to be assessed for the construction and maintenance of the meeting-house and for the salary of the minister. The church— the covenanted body of those admitted to the Lord's table and who were subject to church discipline—was a much smaller number than the whole body of inhabitants of town or parish.

For obvious reasons, the church members would often be more concerned to maintain standards of theological orthodoxy than the inhabitants at large. Hence the liberalism that came to be known as Unitarianism tended to develop in the large ecclesiastical community of the parish rather than in the smaller ecclesiastical community of the church. In such cases, the church declined in importance, and the parish became the true religious community. The covenant, with its creedal coloration, tended to be associated with orthodoxy, while some liberals made it a mark of their liberalism that their religious organizations no longer used covenants.

The organizing function performed by covenants was not abolished by disuse of the term, however. Substitutes began to appear, such as "bond of union" or "bond of fellowship." One formulation adopted in a number of Unitarian churches was composed by Charles C. Ames in 1880 for the Spring Garden Church (now extinct) in Philadelphia. His original wording was: "In the freedom of truth, and the spirit of Jesus, we unite for the worship of God and the service of Man." Such a statement is a covenant in everything but name; indeed it is closer in spirit to the primitive covenants of Salem and Boston than to the creedal covenants that had become common in more orthodox circles.

While Ames's bond of fellowship includes words with theological significance, it is not a creedal statement. The operative words are "we unite," not "we believe." The difference is significant. A creedal covenant sets up a test by which the fitness of prospective members may be judged, and some may be denied admission. A non-creedal covenant, such as Ames's bond of fellowship, suggests the purposes of the community of faith, but leaves it to the individual to decide whether to unite. Unitarian Universalists long ago rejected creedal tests for membership as a way to exclude any whose views may be eccentric or even heretical. We have no mechanism by which one seeking to join may be examined or tested by some ecclesiastical authority for orthodoxy of doctrine. The boundary lines of our churches are drawn by many acts of individual choice, not by official judgment.

A bond of union, a bond of fellowship, a covenant, or even a statement of purpose as a preamble to a set of bylaws may be functionally the same thing. But there is something to be said for the word *covenant*, quite apart from the fact of its long currency. It emphasizes that the church is a community of mutual obligation, which involves a sense of commitment. Even the freest of free churches needs that much discipline if it is to last long enough to accomplish anything of value in this world.

Questions for Discussion

1. What are the roots of our practice of congregational polity? Do we maintain this tradition in our practices today, with respect to (1) the meaning of membership, reflected in the act of joining a UU church or fellowship and (2) the relationship among our churches and fellowships?

2. Conrad Wright distinguishes between a creed and a covenant, using the "bond of fellowship" by Charles C. Ames as an example. What is the importance of this distinction to the quest for a non-creedal basis of unity within and among our churches? How does the word *covenant* function in the Principles of the UUA?

3. When the term *covenant* is used in a religious context (church membership, the relation of a congregation and a minister, the relation of marriage partners, the commitment of congregations to each other in forming the UUA), does it have a sacred dimension—that is, beyond a sense of contractual agreement, does it bear a transcendent or non-manipulable meaning?

From Cage to Covenant

James Luther Adams

Editor's Note. *Based on historical analysis, James Luther Adams enumerates the five ingredients of a covenant that are relevant to liberal religion today. Adams is generally regarded as the most distinguished liberal religious ethicist and theologian of the twentieth century. He taught at the University of Chicago Divinity School, Meadville Lombard, Andover Newton Theological School, and finally, Harvard Divinity School, from which he retired as professor of ethics and theology. His numerous publications include three books of essays edited by his former student, George Kimmich Beach.*

We generally characterize liberal religion's attitude of mind as a critical stance before mere tradition, impatience with creeds delivered once and for all, the rejection of coercion in religion, freedom of conscience, open-mindedness, tolerance, and the liberation of the human spirit from heteronomous authorities. Beautiful attitudes! But attitudes alone do not make or change history. The road to hell is paved with good attitudes. They require institutional embodiment. Indeed, the liberal attitudes mentioned appeared initially in the seventeenth century in connection with a power struggle undertaken in order to change social structures. This struggle was a revolutionary institutional struggle, a struggle against the cage of centralized power in church and state and economic order.*

Reprinted by permission from James Luther Adams, *The Prophethood of All Believers,* edited and with an Introduction by George K. Beach (Boston, Beacon Press, 1986). Copyright by George K. Beach.

*In a famous passage at the end of his *The Protestant Ethic and the Spirit of Capitalism,* first published in Germany in 1904–1905, Max Weber refers to the modern system of industrial production as an "iron cage." See Adams's essay "The Protestant Ethic and Society: Max Weber," in his *On Being Human Religiously,* George K. Beach, Ed. (Boston: Beacon Press, 1976), p. 181.

Congregational polity was the new conception of a covenanted church that gave form to this struggle, a polity separating the church from the state, placing responsibility upon the members (the consent of the governed), and giving rise to a self-governing congregation. But during the past century our society has been moving in the opposite direction, in the direction of a new centralization of power in mammoth bureaucratic government and industry, the fragmentation of responsibility, retreat into privatized religion—all of this in a world of massive poverty and hunger. In the nineteenth century liberal religion promoted these tendencies by emphasizing an atomistic individualism that in a technological society produced the modern industrial corporation with its oligopoly and with even greater power than the government. A major question today in a world of multinational corporations is how to achieve a separation of powers and consent of the governed, a self-governing society in the midst of corporate structures that are rapidly becoming a new cage. So we have moved from cage to cage.

It may well be that we should consider as our intellectual agenda the devising of a doctrine of the church and a theology or philosophy that has an institutional thrust that deals with these issues, not as though the issues were settled, but rather in recognition that within our liberal churches we will see more and more (as we saw in the New Deal) a confrontation, a tension between different social philosophies, the one appealing to the liberalism of an earlier epoch and the other appealing to a new meaning for consent of the governed.

The latter is a new demand for legitimation, that is, the development of responsible corporate policies. In that connection, the doctrine of covenant may be a conception to which we should give systematic consideration, for the sake of the revision of that covenant insofar as it did not in earlier days concern itself with communal responsibility in the economic sphere. Especially important is a reconsideration of that covenant in light of the remarkable biblical scholarship of the last twenty years regarding covenant.

What are the major ingredients of a covenant? With this, I conclude. Five points:

1. Human beings, individually and collectively, become human by making commitment, by making promises. The human being *as such*, as Martin Buber says, is the promise-making, promise-keeping,

promise-breaking, promise-renewing creature. The human being is the promise maker, the commitment maker.

2. The covenant is a covenant of being. It is a covenant with the creative, sustaining, commanding, judging, transforming powers, which may be interpreted theistically or nontheistically, humanistically. In a religious covenant, the orientation is to something we cannot control but something upon which we depend, even for our freedom. Jonathan Edwards called it the "covenant of being."

3. The covenant is for the individual as well as for the collective. Much of the new scholarship on the Old Testament shows how this is true in regard to the Ten Commandments. The individual as well as the collective is brought into the covenant; the individual is brought out of separateness into covenant. So it is for the individual as well as for the collective. We are responsible not only for individual behavior but also for the character of the society and the love and preservation of nature.

4. The covenant responsibility is especially directed toward the deprived, whether these be people suffering from neglect and injustice or those who are caught in the system that suppresses them—that suppresses their own self-determination. It is the gap between covenant and system, between ideal and behavior, that creates deprivation and makes it difficult for a top flight executive, for example, to speak out in public regarding his or her dissident convictions.

5. The covenant includes a rule of law, but it is not fundamentally a legal covenant. It depends on faithfulness, and faithfulness is nerved by loyalty, by love. Violation of the covenant is a violation of trust. What holds the world together, according to this dual covenant then, is trustworthiness, eros, love. Ultimately the ground of faithfulness is the divine or human love that will not let us go. Here we see the theological basis for accountability, by persons and by the church. This may be the fundamental intellectual agenda for today: a *doctrine of the covenant* whether it be given that name or not.

Some such doctrine as this with its decisive element of individual responsibility connected with corporate responsibility is surely high on the agenda if, after having been emancipated from the old cage of domination, we are to cope with the new cage of centralized, bureaucratic power.

Questions for Discussion

1. James Luther Adams is "impatient" of the "beautiful attitudes" which have characterized liberal religion insofar as they have remained attitudes only. Why?

2. What is the "intellectual agenda" Adams would press upon Unitarian Universalists? This essay was originally written in 1977; do you think his agenda has made some headway among us in the twenty-plus years since, for example, the UUA Principles statement which says, "We covenant . . . "?

3. Discuss each of the five ingredients of a covenant outlined by Adams. What do these points say about our understanding of Unitarian Universalism today?

The Web

Bernard Loomer

Editor's Note. We now turn from the past to the future. The following essay is the first of three that look forward, offering new visions of the "city set on a hill." Here, Bernard Loomer theologizes about the Web of Life, that infinitely complex reality parallel to the Kingdom of God as "discovered" by Jesus. Loomer maintains that we do not need a personal God to experience forgiveness and connectedness. We are related to each other through the Web and to the Web through each other. In the Web, power is always mutual—it is giving and receiving. We strive to achieve Loomer's vision through performing works of mutual love and forgiveness. Loomer served as professor and dean of the University of Chicago Divinity School, and then as professor and for a time acting dean at the Graduate Theological Union in Berkeley, of which Starr King is a component. A Baptist theologian, Loomer gave informal Sunday seminars at the First Unitarian Church of Berkeley, where his second wife, Jeanne Wennerstrom Loomer, was very active. He ultimately joined the church before his death in 1985. This essay was excerpted from a monograph of his seminars that was published by the Berkeley church and is included here with the permission of its trustees.

Jesus has been accorded many titles. He has been called Savior, Leader, Shepherd, Counselor, Son of God, Messiah. But his intellectual gifts have not been recognized (even when the term *intellectual* has been more carefully defined). It was he who discovered what he called the Kingdom of God—what I call the Web of Life—surely one of the great intellectual and religious ideas of the Western world.

As I define it, the Web is the world conceived as an indefinitely extended complex of interrelated, interdependent events or units of reality. This includes the human and non-human, the organic and inorganic levels of life and existence. Let's begin with the notion of the Web—or the Kingdom, if you wish—and see how all the things we have been talking about are tied into this conception one way or another: the doctrines of forgiveness, repentance, responsibility, gratitude, sin, transformation, power, and the rest. These conceptions all refer to dimensions of the Web.

Sin is a distortion of our relations to God and to each other. Forgiveness is a restoration to those relationships. In sinful acts we act against the Web of Life. In seeking repentance we open ourselves to the forgiveness that is already there, as a fundamental condition of life. We make ourselves accessible to it, or it accessible to us. We are related to each other through the Web. Those others have free choice as to whether they will accept our forgiveness or not. In all cases we are trapped within an inescapable web of connectedness.

The belief that the Web is impersonal still does not deny forgiveness. We don't need a personal God in order to experience forgiveness and to be restored to a connectedness. Connectedness can be to the whole and to the other person. We are related to each other through the Web and to the Web through each other.

In a real sense you cannot fully forgive yourself. You are a social individual. You are a singular self within a social web. Another has to be involved—at least one other. Your being restored requires an action on the part of that other. You cannot restore yourself simply by your own attitudes and actions. Yet an act of individual acceptance is always involved in forgiveness and repentance. If you cannot forgive yourself, you are denying your own worth and also that of others, and cannot accept the forgiveness of others or of the Web.

We start with the notion of the Web as a world in which the entities in it, including the people, are bound together as interrelated. We are dependent on each other, and yet each claims a kind of independence from all that goes on. The higher one goes in the evolutionary scale, the greater the concern for independence, but one never loses the sense of dependence on the others within the context of an environment in which one lives and moves and has his or her being.

In this sense there is no such thing as a self-made person or a self-made jellyfish or a self-made anything. Everything that exists has contributed to its own existence in part. Everything that exists has been contributed to by the context out of which it has emerged.

If all the creatures that exist were capable of worship, we would all begin each day with a sense of gratitude to the environment on which we are so dependent, from which we draw resources, and to which we make our own contributions, large or small. The Web, in this sense, is not only the gene pool. It is the pool of all that we are, the carrier of all values. What happens in a community, large or small, is important for each one of us, whether or not we are aware of the degree to which we draw strength and sustenance from this environment. We are born or created as members of a Web of interconnections from which there is no escape and on which we are dependent and in which we live out our days. This is a given, not a created condition. It is a given condition. I stress this. I cannot document this in the Gospels and I sometimes have the impression that Jesus himself was somewhat taken aback at times by the simplicity and yet the immensity of his own discovery. This is a given condition. This is not something that has evolved. Our understanding of it has evolved, but the condition itself is a given. This is point one.

Point two, the implications for the self, can be seen quite readily. On the one hand the self is a social self, on the other a singularized, unique individual. The person is both of these at the same time. The person is never one without also being the other, although we may tend to emphasize one dimension more than the other. The nature of human individuality motivates us to deny or resist the very network of dependence and interrelatedness from which we have emerged. It is a fascinating and endless story. The fact of becoming individuals, at least in Western society, causes us to move almost inevitably against that very foundation condition of the world that is necessary for our being in this interrelated world. We are motivated to think that what we achieve is our own doing and we are rightfully proud of it. In all kinds of ways we tend to overemphasize the notion of responsibility at the expense of gratitude. In our minds there is something admirable about the individual who wants to make his or her contribution. There is also something "brattish" about "by myself, by myself, let me do it by myself."

The third point is that since we tend to prize our sense of individuality as an independent self, which often leads to egoism, we have one of the reasons Jesus stressed the two fundamental requirements of repentance and the forgiveness of sins as important conditions of the Kingdom. We also tend to move against the Web, with at least an implied denial of our dependence.

You cannot forgive yourself unless you forgive the other also. You cannot forgive the other unless you also forgive yourself. I think at points we may tend to make a sharp distinction between ourselves and the world. We may then feel that we can forgive ourselves and leave the world intact without bothering about the question of whether we should do anything about the world. I think that this is a mistaken notion, that we probably kid ourselves in thinking we can forgive ourselves without dealing with the communal roots in which our sinfulness is always embedded. It isn't embedded simply within me, nor is yours embedded simply within you. It is embedded within you but it is also embedded within your environment, community, and society. This is why sin is not simply an act or a series of acts. It is, on the one hand, a disposition of the soul. On the other hand, speaking as a rule, it is a structure within things, which is one of the reasons evil is so strong.

So just as we are not individuals and in isolation and apart from this community in which we live, so we cannot live a life of trust, repentance, or forgiveness by ourselves, singularly. A sense of responsibility that is not closely tied in with the sense of trust makes for pride. Responsibility that is not tied in with and does not live with its counterpart called gratitude or thankfulness makes for pride—pride in oneself. I use the words *trust* and *gratitude* in the sense of saying thank you to some other reality for what you have received. It is an acknowledgment that the other, who exists in his or her right, has taken the time and energy to enter your life and has offered you a gift that you are free to accept or not. You acknowledge your thanks even if you decide not to make use of the gift. A sense of responsibility without being tied in with this sense of gratitude makes for pride. Pride, up to a point, is a very necessary element in self-worth. There is no self-worth without some measure of pride. But pride, beyond a certain point, becomes an overevaluation of the self. This becomes estrangement, wherein pride means you gain your status always at someone else's expense. Your foot is in someone else's face. You evaluate yourself "up" by putting someone else "down."

Therefore, power that is most deeply consonant with the nature of the Web has to be mutual in its character, in contrast to the traditional notion of power. Unilateral power, which essentially is a masculine version of power, is wrongheaded. Yet, we had no intellectual corrective (except the traditionally classical notion of love) to counteract the one-sidedness of power.

This means that love as mutuality was not regarded as a high kind of love. It was always thought that the highest form of love was a love that was completely self-forgetful, that involved a total commitment to the other, a concern for the other with no thought of oneself. I think this is due in part to the equally one-sided conception of power, wherein power means that you are the only one who counts and others exist only as means to your chosen end.

Under the notion of the Web or the Kingdom, power in the deepest sense is always mutual. It is a giving and a receiving. It is influencing and being influenced. When you have one without the other there is an unbalanced, one-sided, incomplete kind of relationship going on. This is one of the ways that men particularly under the dominance of the traditional conception of power have been ill trained to develop religiously. It is impossible to develop to great maturity religiously under the domination of this kind of power. This may be one of the reasons that wherever you have a great male religious leader, strong feminine elements are manifested to overcome the imbalance of the masculine conception of the nature of power.

The final point concerns the concept of transformation or surrender. One does not surrender to other finite objects similar to oneself. This is idolatry. It results in a loss of freedom. One can surrender to that dynamic process of mutuality, thereby increasing the internality between the two or more persons involved. That is to give yourself to the relationship, but not to the elements in the relationship. A person is to love the members of the relationship. But the person is to be committed to the relationship. An internal mutual relationship is one in which both are affected. The limits of being affected are without bounds. In the traditional notion of the relationship between people and God, the relationship was external as far as God was concerned since God could influence people without being influenced Himself. On the other hand, the relationship was internal as far as humans were concerned since they were influenced.

Questions for Discussion

1. How does Bernard Loomer's image of the Web (or Kingdom of God) help us make use of religious concepts such as sin and repentance? Can it be used to reinterpret other traditional concepts, radical individualism, for example?

2. Loomer contrasts the idea of "love as mutuality," which he affirms, with the idea of love as "completely self-forgetful." The

latter seems related to the ideas of "unconditional" love or self-sacrificial love, in which concern for self is denied. How is his concept related to his ideas of power as relational (power with) rather than one-sided (power over)?

3. Why do you think the affirmation of "the interdependent web of all existence of which we are a part" has risen to such prominence among Unitarian Universalists in recent years?

Liberating Religious Individualism

Fredric John Muir

Editor's Note. Fredric John Muir finds his vision of the future by switching paradigms. He casts aside radical individualism as a transient belief that's misled liberal religion in this century. Instead, Muir posits a permanent guiding myth: a vision of a truly pluralistic liberal religion that will liberate us to covenant and work in community for social change. Muir received an M.Div. degree from Union Theological Seminary and a D.Min. from Wesley Theological Seminary. Following a seven-year ministry in Maine, he has been minister of the Unitarian Universalist Church of Annapolis, Maryland, since 1983. This essay is reprinted, in slightly edited form, from The Transient and Permanent in Liberal Religion *(Skinner House Books, 1995).*

No doubt, an age will come in which ours shall be reckoned a period of darkness when we groped for the wall but stumbled and fell, because we trusted a transient notion, not an eternal truth; an age when temples were full of idols, set up by human folly.[1]

Theodore Parker

REACHING AN IMPASSE

The scene is as recurrent and predictable as a New England town meeting. At this congregational meeting, as at most others, the arguments reflect an ardent, uncompromising belief in individualism. The topic under debate was banning smoking in the church building.

The first several people to speak suggested that smoking is bad—for the smoker as well as those in the area. It simply did not make sense to smoke. Another person rose to say that whether it was good or bad, smokers had the responsibility to go along with the group, whatever the vote might be. She seemed to have been assuming a ban. Finally, some of those opposed to the ban spoke, interestingly, none of them smokers. "I want to defend the right of those who do smoke, to smoke," one of them said. "Since when have we been in the business of telling people what they can and cannot do?" There was some applause and then another supporter of smokers' rights spoke. "We've always protected the rights of the person here, and I don't want to start taking away those rights now. I don't like smoking either, but if allowing it is what will keep us free, then I want the ban voted down." The debate continued for another fifteen minutes and then the vote came: fifty-five for, and two against.

This congregational meeting highlights three forms of individualism. The first, the sociologist Robert Bellah calls biblical.[2] This biblical individualism recognizes the needs of the individual, but also that there are times when every person has a religious (biblical) obligation to go along with the group. In a culture where we believe in the dignity and sacredness of the individual, biblical individualism attempts to appeal to a broader religious context. In this case "it's bad to smoke" connotes a sense of immorality. To be a good person, a religious person, would be to conform and to refrain from smoking.

The second form is described as civic individualism and is characterized by a straightforward call to do what is best for the group without direct appeal to the divine. Here the argument shifts from theology and morality to civic responsibility. Civic individualism emphasizes the needs of the group and places the individual good within the context of a common good. This is essentially the utilitarian ideal that has shaped much modern ethical thought.

The third form of individualism found in the congregational meeting is modern individualism. It holds that the individual must always take precedence over the group. Although it did not win in this meeting, this is the form of individualism that has taken over our contemporary American culture. Bellah explains, "There are both ideological and sociological reasons for the growing strength of modern individualism at the expense of the civic and biblical traditions. Modern individualism has pursued individual rights and individual autonomy in ever new realms."

Profound conflicts exist among these forms of individualism. Robert Bellah believes the differences have generally been ignored in our times because at their core all three philosophies "stress the dignity and autonomy of the individual." As biblical and civic forms of individualism have acquiesced to the tenets of modern individualism, major problems have emerged. "The question is whether all individualism in which the self has become the main form of reality can really be sustained. What is at issue is not simply whether self-contained individuals might withdraw from the public sphere to pursue purely private ends, but whether such individuals are capable of sustaining either public or private life."

Bellah is not suggesting that we return to the civic and biblical traditions of individualism. He sees that they are also inadequate. Each embodies forms of discrimination not tolerable in contemporary society—sexism, racism, and a loss of individual dignity, as the demands of the group become greater and stronger. The result? We face a profound impasse. Modern individualism seems to be producing a way of life that is neither individually nor socially viable; yet a return to traditional forms would be a return to intolerable discrimination and oppression. The question, then, is whether the older civic and biblical traditions have the capacity to reformulate themselves while simultaneously remaining faithful to their own deepest insights.

Economist Paul King supports Bellah's conclusion, but he asserts that Bellah's analysis is limited.[3] It is not enough to expect an emerging new individualism or a heroism somehow rising out of the old order. Although the strengths of civic and biblical individualism are appealing, they simply carry too many social liabilities to work. King proposes a "heroism" that recognizes the value of individualism yet has its roots in a social basis. He describes an individualism that can grow out of addressing the "tri-lemma" facing the modern middle class.

This "tri-lemma" comes out of an economy that has left the middle class increasingly on a par with the working class and just as vulnerable to poverty as those at the bottom of the economy. On the one hand the middle class is nearly powerless, while on the other it is tacitly expected to participate in the oppression of workers, the unemployed, and the poor. "Finally," King writes, ". . . our structural powerlessness as employees and our individualism create a sense of isolation and meaninglessness, of being unable to change either our vulnerability to or our cooperation in that oppression."

This "tri-lemma" is ingrained in the country's identity and is revealed in our consumerism, nationalism, and religion. We need to address the ways we have come to see ourselves in order to find our identity. Of the first, King asserts, "It was Marx who suggested that 'you are what you do.'" We seem to have changed that into 'you are what you consume.' The second is nationalism. American religions, and even frequently Unitarian Universalists, commonly view religion as interdependent with the American experiment and experience. And third, religion, whether fundamentalist, orthodox, or liberal, has given us an identity in which "the problems and their resolutions are couched in individualistic terms."

The oppressive nature of the "tri-lemma" will increase and debilitate the middle class further as long as the middle class continues to be defined by consumerism, nationalism, and religion. The three forms of individualism critiqued by Bellah, and the three sources of identity put forward by King, are all oppressive and isolating. Nothing about them promotes liberation, community building, empowerment, and interdependency.

The town meeting and the congregational meeting are examples of the pseudo-power King found in middle-class communities. After the smoking debate at the congregational meeting, a member expressed his enthusiasm for what he heard. "Wasn't it great? We have such a variety of people here, such interesting ideas." His remarks add to a commonly expressed belief found in Unitarian Universalist congregations. We have become sanctuaries for religious eclecticism.

This perspective is summarized by the many who repeat, "You can believe anything and be a Unitarian!" This notion is correct in at least one sense: we embrace all three forms of individualism suggested by Bellah. Both Bellah and King conclude that for American society, this embrace has created an impasse.

It has also created an impasse for Unitarian Universalism. In accepting several forms of individualism, even all of them, Unitarian Universalists have avoided making a critical decision, a decision that will have a profound impact on the future. We now stand at a time when we must make a decision for continuing oppression or for liberation. But how will we decide?

IDEOLOGY AND MYTH

"The inherent worth and dignity of every person" is sacrosanct to Unitarian Universalists. To suggest that the needs of the group are just as valid as those of the individual, let alone possibly more valid, is to prompt an inevitable look of disapproval, if not outright hostility. In some circles it can result in accusations of socialism. Where Bellah and others have explained the rise of individualism in American cultures, sociologists Peter Berger and Thomas Luckman provide a framework for understanding how individualism has reached such a near ontological and religious status.

I contend that, though integral to the faith of Unitarian Universalists, individualism is neither inherent nor ontological to our religious or national life. Individualism has achieved this near-sacred status, not because of a God-given character, but as a result of the importance people are willing to give it.

We all have an ideology. There is nothing wrong with this; it is the reality of everyday life. But we do need to be aware that we process information from the perspective of our ideologies and therefore need be aware of what they are. Individualism is an ideology embraced by Unitarian Universalists and, indeed, by American culture for good reasons. Individualism has achieved its near-sacred status because it supports, encourages, and gives meaning to a particular way of life and system of faith. We simply need to remember we have decided to make it so.

While Unitarian Universalists and others have their faith in individualism, some faith traditions place their emphasis elsewhere through the same process of objectivation. For example, theologian Richard Shaull explains that "God exists in us as we develop the right concepts." He suggests that through the process of objectivation, as certain ideas are developed and then projected outward, God is created.

The important thing to remember is there is no such thing as objective reality. Individualism may appear as objective reality because it is such an integral part of the Unitarian Universalist faith system. The appearance of ontological worth creates a tautology that can only preserve the status quo.

We also find ideology embodied in the form of story, our particular myth or myths. "Myths are central in human life," writes Unitarian Universalist minister Alice Blair Wesley. She elaborates: "All people and cultures without exception hold myths to be true. Any who believe that others—less sophisticated—may naively hold myths to be true while they themselves do not, are themselves naive." Psychologist Sam Keen expands on this. "Myth refers to

interlocking stories, rituals, rites, customs and beliefs that give a piv-
otal sense of meaning and direction to a person, a family, a community, or a culture."

As myth, the objectivation of reality that has become ideology can
be retold, rehearsed, and re-presented almost endlessly. As myth, it
can easily be passed on from generation to generation, giving it historical validity that in turn enhances its ontological-like character.
As ideology supports and nurtures the status quo, so too do our
myths.

"A myth involves the conscious celebration of certain values,"
writes Keen, ". . . always personified in a pantheon of heroes. . . . But
it also includes an unconscious, habitual way of seeing things, an
invisible stew of unquestioned assumptions. A living myth, like an
iceberg, is only ten percent visible: ninety percent lies beneath the
surface of consciousness of those who live by it."

Myths are powerful, but not permanent. Individualism as an ideology for Unitarian Universalism is integral to the faith message and
tradition, but it is not absolute or permanent. It exists because we
have chosen it, and we continue to tell the myths that bolster, per-
petuate, and give meaning to Unitarian Univeralist individualism.

This Is Pluralism?

At the same time that Unitarian Universalists tell the myths of individualism, we also talk about pluralism, another integral element of
our faith. Pluralism is an ideal Americans affirm, and it is a principle that Unitarian Universalists agree is not only commendable but
desirable.

In our Principles and Purposes, "We affirm and promote the
inherent worth and dignity of every person . . . acceptance of one
another . . . respect for the interdependent web of all existence of
which we are a part." Pluralism refers to having differences that are
tolerated without loss of individual or group character. Pluralism
means that every person has a right to participate on every level of
societal life regardless of who they are and what they think.
Pluralism in religion indicates a diversity of people and thought all
under the same name.

Pluralism is not the antithesis of individualism. Rather, pluralism
supports individualism. The pluralism and diversity proclaimed as

integral to the Unitarian Universalist faith are based on respect for the inherent worth and dignity of every person. But, we need to ask, what standard is being used to determine these? Indeed, what is the context of this understanding? The United States now has a diversity of cultures unparalleled in its past. This diversity has been the result of rising immigration from Latin America and Asia, in addition to Eastern Europe and the Middle East. The result? "Some Americans who were born in the United States are saying they cannot identify with its prevailing culture," according to historian Andrew Hacker.

While diversity gains momentum on all levels, responses in local communities aren't good. Racism, sexism, and homophobia are at dramatically high levels; the rich and poor grow further apart; there seems to be a strengthening of individual self-protection and isolation.

As diversity races ahead, what about pluralism? What about respect and welcoming of individual differences? As a nation and as a religious movement, there appears the possibility that we will find ourselves on the wrong side of history because we are not prepared for the changes taking place. Unitarian Universalist church historian Conrad Wright discusses in *Walking Together* the need to respond:

> Liberal religion articulated a value system that derived its strength from the social arrangements made possible by the discovery of the exploitable resources of the New World. But those resources were not limitless. The infinity of the private individual was plausible enough on the shores of Walden Pond, when there was no one closer than Concord Village a mile away; it is hollow rhetoric on the streets of Calcutta or in the barrios of Caracas. The progress of humankind onward and upward forever may have seemed an axiom grounded in history to James Freeman Clarke; it seems something less than that to the residents of Middletown, Pennsylvania. The principle of religious toleration was easy for Jefferson, who could not see that it did any injury for his neighbor to say there are twenty gods or no god; but the principles of toleration takes on a sharper edge when the decisive differences are not in the realm of speculative theology, but on the question of apartheid and what it is that others should be forced, despite their opinions, to do about it.

MOVING TOWARD LIBERATION

I believe that liberation theology gives Unitarian Universalists one way to move toward a real pluralism, a living myth. Liberation theology opens a way for the needs of the group while allowing for an individualism that combines the best of the civic and biblical traditions, and even keeps in balance the demands of our modern individualism. Why liberation? We need liberation because we are increasingly empty.

Theologian Charles Bayer refers to a "spiritual ennui" that he believes has become commonplace in American culture. With the routine of daily work and personal calendars reflecting every waking moment planned, Americans settle into bed at night feeling exhausted and empty. Bayer suggests, "Perhaps to a greater degree than any mass culture in history, affluent US middle-class folk have more spare time and more money to use, as they please, but little they can do, no place they can go, and nothing they can buy seems to fill the gray void."

It is no wonder that our churches have members who claim their lives are empty, meaningless, that they feel a dark hole that can't be lighted or filled. They turn to the church for fulfillment. They want to be given the meaning of life just as one might go to the supermarket to be handed packaged meat. Not finding their needs met by an inner strength, some turn to alternatives, work, relationships, alcohol, drugs. These are just the most common choices. These all help to make up the codependencies that have taken over many lives. Some churches support the work of self-help programs: here are opportunities for a handful who have the courage to face their reality. They gather with other codependents to share their experiences. Together, they nurture one another on the road back to recovery.

Another issue interrelated with this spiritual ennui is a life without risk or adventure. Not that one must sign up for Outward Bound or run a marathon, but just to be moved by life, to be passionate about living and compassionate for those with whom we live, could do much. Life is often structured in a way that won't allow for the adventurous, the impromptu, or the unthought-of. After the death of a parishioner, Unitarian Universalist minister David Rankin was moved to write: "A religion that promises a life without tension, a life without conflict, life without suffering is a religion of passivity, a religion of mediocrity, a religion of insignificance. Besides, everything worth doing in the world is a desperate gamble, a game of chance, where nothing is certain."

Spiritual ennui in the form of boredom, codependency, and a lack of adventure dominate the lives of middle-class church members. Liberation from these dehumanizing forces would free people to place their energies outside themselves. But in order to make this final step, a step away from the isolation that comes from modern individualism, there has to be a recognition that individualism is destructive.

This is not to say individualism is bad per se. What I believe is really desired is pluralism. Pluralism embraces the inherent worth and dignity of every person. Pluralism celebrates individualism. But Unitarian Universalism is not pluralistic. We are anything but pluralistic. The membership of Unitarian Universalism is dramatically homogeneous. For the most part we are highly educated, middle class, and white. Our churches are not the environments we say we wish for. Our churches are not at all what we like to think they are.

Moving beyond homogeneity will not be easy, but it will liberate us to a pluralism that can evolve a new myth. Perhaps the creation of a new story is the risk and adventure we need. King suggests, "Theology is most vital and creative when a community begins to recognize that its conception of the world and the actual conditions of historical existence are at odds."

If we will take notice, this is exactly what is happening to us. The Unitarian Universalist myth of individualism is antiquated and running out of steam. It is a transient belief at a time when a permanent belief, a guiding myth, is needed. A transient belief in an isolating and oppressive individualism is not facing the world situation as it is today. Even worse, it is supporting lifestyles that are destructive.

As life around us moves forward at breakneck speed, as personal lives are slipping away, can Unitarian Universalists respond? Wright in *Walking Together* concludes,

> So the fate of religious liberalism rests with us. We may cling to the old paradigm, proclaim individual freedom of belief as an absolute value. . . . Then we may dwindle in numbers and influence until we end up a museum piece, like the Shakers, the Schwenkfelders, and the Swedenborgians. But on the other hand, we may learn how to relate to new social forces, to master a new revival as a segment of the Church Univer-

sal, and we may even contribute something to the humanizing of what threatens to be a far less comfortable world than the one you and I have known.

The time is now at hand when we need to study and critique what Unitarian Universalism stands for. We need to explore the changes and patterns that keep pace with and around us, to dream, articulate, plan, and implement the future course. Our call should be nothing less than the call sounded by Theodore Parker:

> Let then the Transient pass, flee as it will, and may God send us some new manifestation of the Christian faith, that shall stir men's hearts as they were never stirred; some new Word, which shall teach us what we are, and renew us all in the image of God; some better life, that shall fulfill the Hebrew prophecy, and pour out the spirit of God on you men and maidens and old men and children.

NOTES

1. The Theodore Parker quotes are from his landmark sermon, "The Transient and Permanent in Christianity."
2. The Bellah quotes are from *Habits of the Heart: Individualism and Commitment in American Life* by Robert N. Bellah et al. (Berkeley, 1985).
3. The King quotes are from *Risking Liberation: Middle Class Powerlessness and Social Heroism* by Paul King et al. (Atlanta, 1988).

Questions for Discussion

1. Do you agree with the basic assertion of this essay, namely that individualism in American society is a central or underlying social problem? How is this reflected in the economics of the free market and the welfare system? How is it reflected in civil liberties concerns, which may conflict with communal values such as safety? How is it reflected in Unitarian Universalist churches and fellowships?

2. What do you make of Muir's astonishing statement that "there is no such thing as objective reality," that is, an independent or observable reality apart from our mental constructions? Does this concept help mask the false ideology or "myth" of individualism?

3. Do you agree with Muir's suggestion that individualism leads to personal isolation and a condition of "spiritual ennui?" Do you agree that "pluralism [in society] supports individualism"? Under what social or communal conditions?

Rising to the Challenge of Our Times

Rebecca Parker

Editor's Note. Rebecca Parker sets forth the challenge of our times, and she suggests what rising to it will require of us. She discusses why and how we must "place ourselves among the saviors, the redeemers, the leaders in the protection of life." Parker is president of Starr King School for the Ministry, where she teaches theology and religion and the arts. An ordained Methodist minister, Parker holds dual fellowship with the Unitarian Universalist Association. The following essay was originally presented as a talk at the 1997 Annual Meeting of the Thomas Jefferson District. It is published here in edited form by permission of the author.

In my neighborhood in Oakland, California, I sat down recently to list the violent acts within three blocks of our home—only three blocks. Hate words sprayed on the synagogue door during High Holy Days. An elderly Vietnamese American neighbor, a man who came to this country for refuge, shot dead when he opened the door to an intruder who then robbed him of his few possessions. An Ethiopian American killed by a random bullet as he walked along the street; his community mourned publicly, gathering each morning, their keening cry of grief filling the street.

We are all aware of the increasing endangerment to our environment, the rapid loss of species, the infiltration of the world's water system by poisonous chemicals, the growing hole in the ozone layer, the depletion of the rain forests, and the creation of more deserts.

We are aware of the increasing hatred and compartmentalization of human communities. In California we have passed laws to exclude immigrants from participation in public education and health care. In Idaho, Washington, Oregon, Colorado, Florida, and

North Carolina, conservative political forces have repeatedly introduced legislation to constrain the lives of lesbian and gay people. We see these sorrows. And then in the midst of them comes an ugly analysis saying the spiritual crisis in America, the rise of violence, the disruption of our sense of common life, and the feeling of lost values are the fault of uppity women who want equality; people of color who want education and employment; lesbian and gay and bisexual and transgendered people who want to live and love honestly; young, poor women who have so little opportunity that the best they can hope for is a child to hold in their arms; artists who too blatantly hold up a mirror to us; and youth who act out the values of self-interested "me-first-ism" they are taught by the dominant culture.

According to this ugly so-called analysis, the cure for America's "sickness of soul" is to lock up more criminals, cut off the poor from human caring, shut the doors to immigrants, reverse social policies liberals have advocated, and refuse to fund the arts. No nation was ever healed by shutting the door on those whose presence it fears. Such action has been the source of the greatest tragedies in history. If we think similar tragedies are not possible in our nation, our eyes and hearts are not wide open.

Our times ask something of us. A friend of mine says, "Everyone likes to have the best—the *best*—asked of them." We are living in a time when the best that is asked of us is far beyond what we have thought we are capable of or would need to do. I believe that, in rising to the occasion of what is asked of us, we will discover a depth of strength and a richness of love and courage we did not know could be claimed or achieved. For in rising to the challenge of our times, we move into a mystery of life at a depth we had not known was available to us.

THE WORK OF PROPHETIC WITNESS

Our times ask us to exercise our capacity for prophetic witness. By prophetic witness I mean our capacity to see what is happening, to say what is happening, and to act in accordance with what we know. In his essay, "The Fire Next Time," James Baldwin says:

This is the crime of which I accuse my countrymen, for which I and history will never forgive them: that they have

destroyed and are destroying hundreds and thousands of
lives and do not know it and do not want to know it.

Prophetic witness is the voice, the presence, the person able to
name those places where we resist knowing what needs to be
known. It brings to our attention the places of silence and denial
where we are closing our eyes to what is happening, allowing ourselves to be anesthetized, and ignoring that which the world is
telling us when we pay attention. Silence and denial create the environment in which violence and evil flourish.

But to see what is happening, to say what is happening, and then
to *act* in accord with what we know is no simple task. It means
breaking through our own silences, our own numbness, to face fully
what is going on. Joanna Macy teaches a course at Starr King School
for the Ministry called Despair and Empowerment. After many
years of social justice work, particularly on behalf of the environment, she's come to the conviction that it is mainly numbness that
keeps us from doing what we need to do to save the planet.

We can recite the litany about the rain forests and the disappear-
ance of species and the hole in the ozone layer. But to feel viscerally
how much peril we and the earth are in is something we cannot
accomplish. We notice only from the corner of one eye. Joanna asks,
What keeps us from being able to see? Her answer is: our despair.
We cannot be present to the depth of our own grief and fear. She says
that, before we can move into empowerment, we must become capable of moving through our grief, our tears. This is more than we
thought would be asked of us. But we have to have the strength to
grieve. Only then do we become capable of fully seeing. Only then
can we fully speak and act in accord with what we know. This is
how prophetic witness works.

Hanna Arendt begins her essay, "The Life of the Mind," by telling
the story of her effort to understand how Nazism succeeded in
Germany. She attended the Eichmann trials in Jerusalem and
watched as witnesses described the part they played in the death
camps. After watching witness after witness, she came to the conclusion that the explanation for their tragic and horrible acts was not
profound malevolence. It was lack of thinking. Those who built and
operated the death chambers, ordered and carried out orders for
atrocities, shared a common characteristic. That common characteristic was flatness. People blandly reported turning on the gas as if

they had no feeling, even in retrospect, for what that act meant. She said it was as if they had lost the ability to connect their actions to the consequences of their actions. There was a numbness, a non-seeing, a non-feeling, a non-knowing, a non-thinking.

To think is to see the relationships, to know that if we keep fertilizing the soil with chemicals that sink into the water table and then destroy the birds' ability to lay eggs, birds disappear. To think is to see relationships. The prophetic witness thinks and feels. Our best thinking and feeling is asked of us now.

We need recovery from numbness and thoughtlessness to deal with racism. Baldwin's point, in part, is that racism in the United States has flourished because of white people's numbness and inability to see its complex structural reality. In the Thomas Jefferson District, consciousness has been raised on this matter—as it was for our whole movement. At the General Assembly in Charlotte, the district hosted a Thomas Jefferson Ball, inviting people to come dressed in period costumes. African American Unitarian Universalists asked, Shall we come wearing chains? Those of us who are white found ourselves asking, How could we have been so unthinking? How did we fail to remember that Jefferson owned slaves? Baldwin writes:

> Before [we] can look forward in any meaningful sense [we] must first . . . take a long look back. . . . Neither whites nor blacks have the faintest desire to look back; but the past is all that makes the present coherent and further . . . the past will remain horrible for exactly as long as we refuse to assess it honestly.

Honest assessment of the past involves not forgetting the history of slavery and not denying that all of us are implicated in this history. Not one among us who is white has not inherited white privilege and white advantage. We do not turn that fact around by disassociating ourselves from slaveholders. Disassociating ourselves can leave us with the illusion that we have done something, when we have only acted to shore up our identity as the pure people, untainted by the sinners.

I am learning to see that what leads me as a white person to forget or separate myself from the realities of racism is that I am preoccupied with the desire for innocence. I want to be free from guilt, to not have my hands dirty, to not be mixed up with anything ugly. The pursuit of purity is the heart of white supremacism. We think we can achieve purity by disconnecting with those we find unacceptable.

Unitarian Universalists in the Thomas Jefferson District have considered whether to change their district's name. The decision warrants careful thinking. If we renounce the name of Thomas Jefferson, how will this act be different from the pattern of white supremacy? Would a name change be more than an attempt to purify the community of association with the unclean? Further, how shall we Unitarian Universalists maintain a commitment to face history honestly and make justice in the present? How shall we do more than wash our hands of one great man simply to redeem another moment our liberal movement forgot when we acted out of denial?

These are not easy questions. Prophetic witness keeps us alert to history and to the current consequences of history. It asks us to redeem history, not in a search for personal freedom from guilt, but in the search for a quality of common life in which none flourishes because another suffers. Prophetic witness asks more of us than that we wash our hands. It asks that we roll up our sleeves and work.

The Work of Remembering Who We Are

There is a second task asked of us in these times: We must find ways to access knowledge that is in danger of being lost. You could say our task is the preservation of endangered knowledge. We're living in an age when our daily life is dominated by the marketplace. The marketplace says we are nothing more than self-interested individuals with an insatiable need for goods. When the marketplace dominates, knowledge of other dimensions of being human gets lost.

The awareness that our intimate relationships are filled with meaning, that we are connected to and depend on the earth, that we have interests transcending our own personal lives—these dimensions are not factored into the values of the marketplace. The dominant, dominating world view of our culture is interested solely in how we are doing business. It's not that business cannot be done in an ethical way, but the way this culture is doing business values profits and the bottom line at any cost and exclusively defines us as self-interested individuals. The marketplace has turned many of us into consuming machines and, in the process, our lives are made small and trapped.

Almost all of us know the meaning of life cannot be found in this narrow, manic way. We know this, but it is hard to remember. It is hard to disconnect ourselves from this dominant activity. My teacher, John Cobb, in the mature years of his career as a theologian, is putting all his energy into analyzing and critiquing the operating assumptions of our increasingly globalized economy. He is doing this because he has come to believe that our current economic system has become The Major World Religion. We must resist this devaluing of ourselves and the earth on which we live by doing the work of remembering who we are. I commend to you two spiritual practices as pathways to the preservation of this knowledge.

The first is keeping the Sabbath. To keep the Sabbath is a radical act of resistance in a culture that has lost track of the meaning of life. Keeping the Sabbath, we give ourselves room for the things that have real meaning: our families, our friends, the sweetness in the air when the tulips are in bloom, time to pray and reflect and give thanks and hear the wisdom of the ages. Keeping the Sabbath, we become capable of entering a profound and sustained engagement with a culture of which we are members and which needs our creative witness and work for change.

The fullness of who we are is endangered knowledge in this culture. The knowledge that we are at risk of forgetting or never coming to know deeply is that to be a human being is to live in a world that has deeply provided for us, a world of which we are stewards. So I commend to you tithing, a spiritual practice that will teach you to know yourself as a person who has received from life and has much to give. We must act in accordance with what we know: that we have received abundantly in our lives and that our presence matters. We are people who are a blessing.

THE WORK OF ENDURING
THE SHAMANISTIC JOURNEY

The third thing that is asked of us in these times is to learn to endure the shamanistic journey. I mean by the shamanistic journey the journey in which one moves into the places of grief and pain, silence, denial, loss, disintegration, and breakdown. In that descent into the underworld—as archetypal psychology would name it—in the place of grief and sorrow we face how much danger there is, how much loss has already occurred. There we discover afresh our capacity to feel, our longing and passion for life, our heart of courage, and our vision for what can be.

The shamanistic journey is the ability to *move through*. It is the kind of transformation in which we let go of what has been, pass through loss, and enter new knowledge, new nourishment, new vision and discovery. Religious communities symbolically reenact such journeys. This is the importance of ritual in our lives. Rituals teach our souls the passages we will be required to move through in our living.

For example, the Jewish tradition of the Passover journey is a form of the shamanistic journey. It marks departure from an established, unjust world into a wilderness of lostness and fear and hunger, to a revelation of new ways of living discovered in all the terror and glory of Mount Sinai, and in the midst of the squabbling conflicts among the people. The people traverse the desert and cross the river into new land. That is a collective shamanistic journey.

In the Christian tradition, each year a shamanistic journey is recalled in the story of the death and resurrection of Jesus. The ritual recalls our human capacity to push the presence of the sacred out of the world, to break ties with one another, to break faith and run away from the best that is asked of us. It recalls the dreadful ability to fail one another and then it recalls to us the abiding presence of grace and mercy that calls us *to* each other and *to* ourselves and *to* holiness itself and promises life beyond—life beyond the ways in which we violate and destroy the gifts of life.

The shamanistic journey is narrated also in Native American traditions and in myths and ritual practices from around the world. As Unitarian Universalists, we are willing to open ourselves to wisdom from many sources. But this wisdom in particular, this kind of journey, we especially need to pay attention to now. We need to pay attention not only by rehearsing the stories, but by allowing ourselves to enter into the experience. This means living a worship life that moves beyond our heads into our hearts and into our bodies. And in this worship life we begin to learn what we must in actuality do in our individual lives.

The shamanistic journey is important because we are living in a culture that must stop being the way it is and allow itself to be transformed. We cannot go on as we are. We know this. Ways of life we are all enmeshed in—economic systems, our whole patterns of living, our whole established world—are not adequate for the quality of life we know we ourselves capable of and that we want for the earth's people. We must become capable of offering religious leadership to a society called to change its fundamental ways of living. We must become people who know personally the pathway of conversion, and people who can bear witness to and keep company with a culture that will do everything it can to resist this passage.

We must offer to the larger society the leadership to move and we must recognize others who already carry the wisdom of this kind of passage. There are people who carry the wisdom of the shamanistic journey, especially among those currently targeted as most dangerous to our society. There are leaders in the black church, among lesbian, gay, bisexual and transgender people, among Jews, among women, in the child in us and among us, among the old, and among the artists. Those most at risk in our culture have been rightly named most dangerous because they know a way through transformation. It is our responsibility as a religious community to offer sanctuary and shelter to the religious visionaries—people of soul who know the way ahead. We have performed this service before. Sometimes, as Unitarian Universalists, we ourselves have been such witnesses. But when we cannot do it ourselves, we are capable of recognizing and supporting the saints, the great souls, the sages, the religious leaders among us.

CONCLUSION

These reflections began with an enumeration of ugly acts of violence. In the end, it is not ugliness that gives us the energy to rise to the challenge of our times. It is beauty. Yes, we are enraged by the destruction of life, but our sustained action is impelled by our experience of life's sweetness. James Baldwin looked at all the pain done to his people and its consequences in the world, but his ultimate question was "What do we do with all this beauty?"

This is the way it was with Moses. Moses was out doing his job one day, minding his own business in the pasture, keeping watch over the flocks by day, when he saw the bush on fire! You've seen it. I saw it one morning as I watched the dawn light skim the tops of the cedars, transfusing the mists over the silver water. You've seen it in the face of a newborn child or your lover's eyes in a moment of intimacy. You've seen it in the rain forest or the high ridges of the Smokey Mountains. You've seen it in the middle of a church service when people were singing, or felt it in the silence. It has whispered to you in a tender voice. It has held you and stopped you in your tracks.

And you, too, have asked, "What do we do with all this beauty?" When Moses saw it, the voice from the bush said, "You must go back to Egypt where I have seen my people in their travail. You must lead them to freedom."

Moses, of course, said what anyone would: "Ask someone else to do this!"

But the voice was insistent. "No, you must go. You must offer this leadership."

And Moses wrangled with God and said, "Look, my brother Aaron would be much better, okay? The Quakers would be much better. The progressive Catholics would be much better. The reconstructionist Jews, they could do this!"

The voice was insistent. "No. You must go. You must do this."

Beauty confronts us with the requirement that we place ourselves among the saviors, the redeemers, the leaders in the protection of life. Once you have seen the bush on fire, you are not going to get out of the assignment unless you close your eyes to the beauty. But if you have seen, if you have taken off your shoes, tasted the blackberries, and felt the tenderness of love, if you have seen how the full force of soul is in each child that comes into this world, you either have to close your eyes or go back to Egypt and set the people free.

More is asked of us than we have imagined. The blessing of life is that it will not let us go until we ourselves have offered the blessing we have to give. As Rumi said, "Let the beauty we love be what we do." Let us, in faith with all those who have gone before us, place ourselves among those who bless the world. Amen.

Questions for Discussion

1. Parker says, "Our time asks us to exercise our capacity for prophetic witness." What prophetic witness are you making, and what courage or confidence or concern enables you to make it? What prophetic witness do you feel you should be making, and what keeps you from doing so?

2. Parker says that "the third thing that is asked of us in these times is to learn to endure the shamanistic journey." What does she

mean? Have you experienced such a journey in your personal life? In the ritual life of your religious community?

3. How might "our capacity for prophetic witness" and learning "to endure the shamanistic journey" affect your congregation's vision and covenant?

Covenants
Old and New

Walter P. Herz

Editor's Note. You've looked into the future. Now it's time to get down to work in the present. The following essay is the first of five designed to help you (and your congregation) begin to structure or renew your vision and covenant. Here I provide samples of covenants from a few of our older congregations—in both original and present manifestations. You will note immediately the immense variety. I thank the churches for providing this material.

This section includes the original and present covenants from seven of our churches founded before 1870. The seventeenth, eighteenth, and nineteenth centuries are represented, and there is substantial geographic spread. These choices represent only a few of the countless covenants used over a period of 390 years in liberal religious congregations in North America.

A few observations about this small sample are appropriate. The earliest covenants are non-creedal and clearly express the relationship of the congregants and their promised behavior toward one another. In the late eighteenth century and throughout much of the nineteenth, covenants tended to be creedal with little, if any, direct emphasis on expected behavior. The contemporary covenants are incredibly diverse in both form and content.

Virtually all of the churches whose covenants are shown had a number of covenants between their original and current ones. Covenants were called such with less and less frequency during the nineteenth century. By the twentieth century, terms such as *affirmation, bond of union, purpose, mission statement,* and *preamble to the constitution* or *bylaws* were more generally in favor. They are all used today.

First Parish Church in Plymouth, Massachusetts

1620
We, the Lord's free people, have joyned ourselves into a church estate, in the fellowship of the gospell, to walke in all his wayes, made known, or to be made known, according to our best endeavours, whatsoever it should cost us, the Lord assisting us.

1997
We, as the Lord's free people, join ourselves into a church estate, in the fellowship of the Gospel, to walk in all his ways, made known, or to be made known, unto us, according to our best endeavors, whatsoever it should cost us, the Lord assisting us.

First Parish in Cambridge, Massachusetts

1636
We covenant with the Lord and one with another; and do bind ourselves in the presence of God to walk together in all his ways, according as he is pleased to reveal himself unto us in his blessed word of truth.

1997
(Used as antiphonal reading)
We, the members of the First Church in Cambridge (Unitarian Universalist), covenant to affirm and promote:

- The inherent worth and dignity of every person
- Justice, equity, and compassion in human relations
- Acceptance of one another and encouragement to spiritual growth in our congregation
- A free and responsible search for truth and meaning
- The right of conscience and the use of the democratic process within our congregation and in society at large

The goal of world community with peace, liberty, and justice for all

- Respect for the interdependent web of all existence of which we are a part.
- The living tradition we share draws from many sources; direct experience of that transcending mystery and wonder, affirmed

in all cultures, which moves us to a renewal of the spirit and an openness to the forces which create and uphold life

- Words and deeds of prophetic women and men which challenge us to confront powers and structures of evil with justice, compassion, and the transforming power of love

Wisdom from the world's religions which inspires us in our ethical and spiritual life

- Jewish and Christian teachings which call us to respond to God's love by loving our neighbors as ourselves

- Humanist teachings which counsel us to heed the guidance of reason and the results of science, and warn us against idolatries of the mind and spirit

- The faithful keeping of those who, through many generations, have sought to create in this place a beloved community of memory and hope

- Grateful for the religious pluralism which enriches and ennobles our faith, we are inspired to deepen our understanding and expand our vision. As a free congregation, we enter into this covenant, promising to one another our mutual trust and support.

ARLINGTON STREET CHURCH, BOSTON, MASSACHUSETTS*

1803(?)

In the presence of God and this Church, you profess your belief in the only living and true God and your desire to live according to his will.

You believe that the Scriptures of the Old and New Testament contain the records of God's revelations to mankind, and afford the only perfect rule of faith and practice.

You believe in Jesus Christ, the son of God as he is revealed in the Scriptures;—that he came into the world to be our Teacher, example and Lord;—that he died for our sins and rose again;—and that he is now exalted at God's right hand to be our Mediator and Judge.

---

*The church was originally gathered in 1726. This covenant was adopted on an unknown date during the years William Ellery Channing occupied the pulpit (1803–1842). At that time it was known as the Federal Street Church.

Acknowledging with sorrow that you have sinned, and relying on the assistance of God's spirit, do you now resolve to obey the precepts and to follow the example of Jesus Christ, hoping through him the forgiveness of sins and life everlasting.

1997

We the members of the Arlington Street Church covenant as a free congregation our shared faith in the Principles and Purposes of Unitarian Universalism and the living tradition from which they draw.

Our Congregation

- We are a community of searchers whose paths lead us to the Arlington Street Church.
- We are a safe haven where we accept members and friends where they are.
- We welcome the spectrum of individual and family lifestyles that so enrich our lives.
- We affirm love and openness as the path towards the unity of our many diversities.

Our Ministry

- We celebrate our called ministers and the calling of each of us to minister to each other.
- We value all who work here, members, friends, and staff.
- We treasure our Sunday worship and weekday service through which we serve our neighbors, our city, our nation, and our planet.
- We delight in the music, drama, and art we hear and make throughout the year that enriches our worship and communal life.
- We rejoice in educating our children, our young people, and our adults.

Our Church

- We honor our historic building as the visible center of our programs and our outreach. Our bells ring out for peace and justice and our sanctuary and meeting rooms exist for the gatherings of the larger community seeking open discourse.

Our Beliefs

- As Unitarian Universalists we affirm our individual paths and shared spiritual journeys.
- We strive to communicate clearly our sense of community with each other and in our world.
- We learn from one another.

Faith in Action

- We are an activist church working for social justice, connecting to the wider Unitarian Universalist movement, and reaching out as individuals and in community to churches and groups everywhere.

ALL SOULS CHURCH OF NEW YORK

1821

In the presence of God and in the name of Jesus Christ: We, whose names are underwritten do, by this act, profess our faith in Jesus Christ and our subjection to the laws of his Kingdom. We receive the Scriptures of the Old and New Testament as our rule of faith and guide of life; and in a humble and grateful reliance on the mercy offered for the pardon of our sins, and for assistance in our duties, we take upon ourselves the engagements of the Christian profession. By this transaction, we profess our earnest desire to obtain the salvation made known to us in the Gospel, and our serious purpose to comply with the terms on which it is offered. We promise to manifest our fidelity to our Lord and Master by observing the ordinances which He has appointed, by submission to the laws of Christian Order and by all the offices of Christian fellowship; beseeching the God and Father of our Lord Jesus Christ that, being faithful unto each other and to the great Head of the Church, we may enjoy the consolations of our Religion, and receive its rewards hereafter, through riches of Divine favor manifested by Jesus Christ.

1997

In the freedom of the truth and in the spirit of Jesus we unite for the worship of God and the service of all.

First Unitarian Church of Cincinnati

1830
I believe in the Holy Scriptures as the word of God, and receive them as the proper and only rule of faith and duty. I believe in Jesus Christ as the Son of God, exalted to be a prince and savior, the mediator between God and man, the way, the truth and the life. On His religion I rest my hopes of salvation, His precepts I wish to obey, and I now unite myself to this church, to commemorate His love in the ordinance which He instituted and gave to His disciples, the Lord's Supper. I do this as an expression of my firm faith in the divinity of His religion and my earnest desire to live as His disciple and become through the mercy of God an heir of salvation.

1997
The purpose of this Church is to foster a continuing search for truth, a reverence for the life force, and a respect for the preservation of the dignity of every person as each seeks fulfillment.

First Unitarian Congregation of Toronto

1846
Leading Principles of the Society
The leading principles of this society shall be the maintenance of the free exercise of private judgment in all matters of belief and the rejection of all tests, creeds or formal declaration of opinion.

In all proceedings of this Congregation, it shall be competent to females holding sittings in the church and being regularly enrolled as the holders thereof, to attend all meetings of the congregation, and to exercise the same privileges as members of this society, as are exercised by males.

1997
The Leading Principles of this Congregation
The leading Principles of this Congregation shall be the free exercise of private judgment in all matters of belief. Members of the Congregation, while free to hold diverse beliefs concerning the nature of God, Humanity and the Universe, are each committed to the preservation of personal integrity, the continuing search for truth through the use of critical enquiry, the democratic method in human relations and the obligation to work together with love for the greater good of all.

This Congregation shall be open to all people regardless of race, ancestry, place of origin, colour, ethnic origin, citizenship, sexual orientation, or handicap.

First Unitarian Church of Portland, Oregon

1866

You do, in this solemn presence, give up yourself to the true God in Jesus Christ, and to his people also, according to the will of God, promising to walk with God, and with this Church of his, in all his holy ordinances, and to yield obedience to every truth of his, which has been or shall be made known to you as your duty, the Lord assisting you by his Spirit and grace.

We, then, the Church of Christ in this place, do receive you into the fellowship, and promise to walk toward you, and to watch over you, as a member of this Church, endeavoring your spiritual edification in Christ Jesus our Lord.

1997

Given our long and distinguished history in Portland, we covenant together:

- To create a welcoming community of diverse individuals,
- To promote love, reason, and freedom in religion,
- To foster lifelong spiritual growth, and
- To act for social justice.

Questions for Discussion

1. Why do you think the oldest covenants (dating from the early seventeenth century) are the simplest? Do they include—perhaps surprisingly—the liberal idea of progressive revelation?

2. Many of our churches and fellowships are creating and adopting mission statements. Do you think more should create and officially adopt covenants? Which, if any, of these sample covenants would you take as models?

3. A covenant is an agreement among two or more parties that commits them to certain future actions or relationships. As such it can be secular or religious. Judaism is founded on the idea that

God initiated a covenant with the ancient Israelites, and Unitarian Universalists today would say that they come together to fulfill a sacred or in some sense a profoundly religious purpose. How would you express the sacred or spiritual dimension of the covenant that unites your religious community?

What They Dreamed
Be Ours to Do
Lessons from the History of Covenant

Rebecca Parker

Editor's Note. In her previous essay, Parker said "The blessing of life is that it will not let us go until we ourselves have offered the blessings we have to give." Here, she relates how our heritage of covenant provides us today with the means of offering our blessings and fulfilling the promise of the free church. This edited version of the talk Parker delivered at the 1998 General Assembly is included by permission of the author. Her biographical data can be found preceding "Rising to the Challenge of Our Times."

What shall we promise one another? The history of covenant can help us answer this question.

Covenant, most simply, means "to come together" as we are doing here in this hall of Covenant. ("Convention" is from the same Latin root *con,* meaning "together," and *venire,* meaning "to come.") Covenant, more specifically, means "to come together by making a promise," as when two people promise to love and care for one another.

As Unitarian Universalists, we most often speak of covenant as a verbal statement of promise among individuals who exercise their power to choose, and thus bring community into being. There are historical reasons why we think this way. It is an expression of the dominance of an individualistic understanding of human existence: individual first, then community.

The theological history of covenant has another side, and can be a resource to help us see another way. And we need another way now. The limits of a merely individualistic understanding of human existence are pressing upon us. Our attachment to an economic system that maximizes self-interest has broken our covenant with the earth and with our neighbor. In our religious movement we are grappling with what this means, including taking a hard look at the complicity of our religious tradition in this broken covenant. It is important that we do this. Multiple oppressions that our hearts cry out against—racism, sexism, the neglect of children, and the abuse of the environment—intersect in an economic system whose bottom line is the maximization of self-interest for individuals. This morning I invite you into a theological reflection on covenant-making, turning especially to history as a resource to help us see another way.

WE INHERIT COVENANT BEFORE WE CREATE COVENANT

To begin, a story.

Eight years ago I moved to California to become President of Starr King School for the Ministry. Truth be told, I was feeling proud of myself. Captain of my ship and master of my soul, I had valiantly charted my course to become, first, a cellist, then a minister, and now an educator.

When I arrived in California, I discovered I had a passle of distant cousins I had never met. One of them, my cousin Eldon Ernst, was Dean of the American Baptist seminary at the Graduate Theological Union in Berkeley. He proposed an Ernst family reunion, and so we got together. When we arrived in the driveway of cousin Sally Ernst's home, I got the first introduction to my distant cousins by reading the bumper stickers on their cars. One said, "If you want peace, work for justice." Another, "Teachers do it with class." Another, "Live Music Is Best." And then there was one that said, "If you love Jesus, tithe."

Inside, over Jell-O salad, home-made rolls, and tuna casserole reminiscent of every church potluck I had ever attended, we said hello to one another. Here was Sally, a minister of religious education and a graduate of the Pacific School of Religion. And here was Mike, a professional French horn player and high school music teacher. And Eldon, a seminary dean. And David, a United Methodist parish minister. Every single one of my distant cousins was a musician, or a minister, or a teacher—and several were all three! Not only that, the ministers were all liberal, social-activist types with an intellectual bent. And all the musicians were classical musicians.

Apparently I had never made any choices at all! My life was given to me. I did not make myself. And this is how it is:

We receive who we are before we choose who we will
become.

As human beings, our lives begin and never leave the soil of this earth that shapes us through blood, kinship, genes, culture, associations, social systems, networks of relationships, and extended communities. Even when we do not directly know the people whose lives are linked with ours, our lives unfold in relationship to theirs. This is how it is with covenant as well. We are born into relationships before we shape relationships by our conscious intention.

We inherit covenant before we create covenant.

We do not make ourselves. We are given the gift of life, the gift of the earth that sustains life, and the gift of one another—here, now—and in all the generations leading up to now. As the Brian Wren hymn puts it:

We are not our own,
Earth forms us,
Human leaves on nature's growing vine,
Fruit of many generations,
Seeds of life divine.

Covenant-making must begin with the question, "What have we been given?" "What is the covenant we are already in?"

In 1550, Robert Browne, inspired by the Reformation, drew on the biblical image of promise-making between God and people to propose a revolution in church life. Churches should come into being, he said, as a covenant among persons—not through common assent to a doctrine, or through sacraments administered by priests hierarchically arrayed and apostolically descended. Instead, people should join themselves by a mutual agreement to walk together, to keep Christ's commandments, to choose their ministers and teachers, to put forth and debate questions to learn the truth, and to welcome the voice of protest, complaint, and dissent. Browne hoped there would be a church in which people would mutually agree

"that any might protest, appeal, complain, exhort, dispute, reprove,
. . . watch for disorders, reform abuses, and debate matters."
(Quoted in Woodhouse, *Puritans and Liberty*, p. 73)
  "What they dreamed be ours to do" we sang yesterday morning.
We thought we had made ourselves! Here we are, Mr. Browne, 450
years later. We are the fulfillment of your dream! Our present-day
character was shaped by the vision long ago. We have inherited who
we are. It is important for us to remember this side of things: that we
are first of all relational beings, shaped by history, by a community
of faith. Our exercise of free choice is in the context of relational existence.
  The early theologians of covenantal church life knew this. They
spoke of the Covenant of Grace. They said God, by the workings of
grace, creates the community of regenerated souls. Human action in
making a church covenant merely makes visible what the Creator of
Life has already done by giving human beings the gift of life and
empowering us to be together in freedom and peace.
  Explicit covenant-making is a human response to a gift from a
source larger than ourselves. In our own time, James Luther Adams
has emphasized this. Let us remember his voice:

  Traditionally our churches have been grounded in a covenant
  binding us together . . . but this enterprise of maintaining the
  network is itself not to be understood as simply a human
  enterprise. It is a response to a divinely given creative power,
  a sustaining-power, a community-transforming power. This
  power is ultimately not of our own making. . . . (Adams, *The
  Prophethood of All Believers*, p. 252)

  There is room to imagine this source larger than ourselves in multiple ways: Earth itself, the Spirit of Life, God, the Buddha, nature,
the communion of all souls, universal love. The point is, there is a
power that undergirds our covenant-making that is more than the
power of our will and decision-making. In fact, our covenant-making is a response to this power, a co-working with this power. We
make this response, most fundamentally, not by what we say, but by
what we do—by coming together in peace, committing ourselves to
be co-workers with the source of life. Covenant is, first-most, not a
verbal agreement, but a practice.
  The Cambridge Platform of 1648 defined the principles of
covenantal church life in New England. The Platform states:

. . . real agreement and consent they do express by their constant *practice* in coming together for the public worship of
God, and by their religious subjection unto the ordinances of
God . . . not only by word of mouth, but by sacrifice . . . and
also, sometimes, by silent consent, without any writing, or
expression of words at all. (Cambridge Platform, Chapter IV,
Section 4, "Voluntary Agreement, Consent or Covenant")

If they say there is no communion without words, tell them, I
have heard that lie before. (Barbara Merritt, quoting Rumi in
the Service of the Living Tradition, June 28, 1998)

The Puritan Richard Mather wrote similarly in 1644:

Covenant may be implied by . . . constant and frequent acts of
communion performed by a company of Saints joined together by cohabitation in towns and villages . . . the falling in of
their spirits into communion in things spiritual. . . . (Quoted
in Woodhouse, p. 301)

What a lovely phrase: "The falling in of their spirits into communion." It is important for us to recover this dimension of
covenant. It is an antidote to our radical individualism. We need this
older sense: Covenant is brought into being by grace and sustained
by practice. Our verbal promises are the frosting on the cake. They
aren't the cake itself. They may help us keep the covenant we are in,
but they are not the covenant itself.

As Rev. Dr. Peter Raible says, "Let us turn more to our act than to
our word to declare our true religion." By our act—for example our
act of being here, our act of worshipping in a Unitarian Universalist
congregation, our act of structuring our life together to give room
for the experience, voice, and vote of each person, our act of joining
together to resist injustice—by these acts, to use Richard Mather's
language, "our spirits have fallen into communion. . . ."

We've fallen into communion with the feisty, free-spirited
Puritans of 450 years ago who advocated freedom of religious conscience and resisted the oppressive powers of church and state.
We've fallen into communion with the people who believe revelation is not sealed. John Robinson's words to the departing Pilgrims
echo in us still, "The Lord hath more truth yet to break forth. . . . I
beseech you remember it is an article of your church covenant that

you be ready to receive whatever truth shall be made known to you. . . . We've fallen into communion with the sweet-spirited Universalists of old, who rejected a notion of God as a tyrant ruling by the threat of hell, and named God as a gracious, creative presence, who saves all through the power of love. We've fallen into communion with the deep-feeling Transcendentalists, insisting that religion cannot be found in the dry bones of the past but must be discovered first-hand.

We've fallen into communion with the Iowa Sisterhood, and all those women and men who have argued and advocated for the rights and full humanity of women. We've fallen into communion with the all-embracing mystics, who see truth manifest in the diverse religious traditions of earth's people and mysteries revealed in the trees and the stars. And, we've fallen into communion with courageous Humanists, who dare to lift up the dignity and strength of human beings, the power and importance of critical reason, in a world that prefers the abrogation of human agency and the uncritical obedience to false gods.

Lives that speak and deeds that beckon.

We live within this communion of souls and receive the beauty given to us by their lives, so closely linked with ours. This is the covenant we are already in. What shall we do with this gift?

WHAT WE HAVE BEEN GIVEN:
A COMMUNITY OF RESISTANCE

I'd like to propose one answer. You may think of others. My suggestions is this: What we are given, most of all, is membership in a community of resistance to oppression. Let us wake up into the dream they dreamed of abundant life for all and, in our time, put into practice the way of life that will embody the realization of that dream. In the words of English Puritan Richard Overton, 1647:

> It is a firm . . . and radical principle in nature, engraved in the
> tables of the heart by the finger of God in creation, for every
> living, moving thing, wherein there is the breath of life, to
> defend, preserve, guard, and deliver itself from all things
> hurtful, destructive and obnoxious thereto, to the utmost of

its power. . . . By all rational and just ways and means possible . . . to save, defend, and deliver [life] . . . from all oppression, violence and cruelty. . . . (Quoted in Woodhouse)

The free church tradition emerged in the sixteenth century as part of a reforming movement that resisted the corrupt hierarchical power of the church and the economic alliance between the feudal aristocracy and the church. The making of church covenants asserted the power of people to determine their own lives, and to choose who would govern them. It was a grass-roots empowerment movement that became a decisive factor in the rise of modern democracy and the emergence of a post-feudal economic system.

In the presence of injustice and oppression, our forbears embraced freedom. They advocated for free speech, dissent, open debate, and tolerance of different opinions in a disciplined search for truth. This free speech was important, not only as an end in itself, but as a means to social change. They challenged economic systems that neglected the poor, justice systems that were unfair, prison systems that were cruel, and economic practices that concentrated wealth in the hands of a few.

The covenant of which we are a part is a tradition that resists oppression by directly challenging the authority of oppressors, acting to remove them from power, and establishing new structures or alternative communities that put what is hoped for into practice. Most importantly, in this covenant, oppression is resisted finally not by argument, not by protest marches, not by the passing of resolutions, but by the practices of covenanted church life.

Betty Reid Soskin, a contemporary Unitarian Universalist community activist, articulates this radical principle this way: "The way to change the world is to be what we want to see." Quaker Jim Corbett, the leader of the Sanctuary movement, speaks of this as civil initiative. Civil initiative, in contrast to civil disobedience (as important as civil disobedience can be), brings about change by proposing and manifesting more than by dismantling and opposing.

Our Puritan forbears resisted oppression by putting into practice a way of life that manifested an alternative to the structures of oppression that dominated their lives. This was the heart of their covenant: to be what they wanted to see, to live as if the day of justice had arrived. They organized their church life to include the free conscience of each individual in a mutual commitment to the common good. They manifested an alternative to the oppressive use of power by a small elite, uninterested in the welfare of all, exercising economic and religious power without consent or accountability. As matters evolved, what the Puritans first practiced in their congregations transformed nations. Puritan scholar A.S.P. Woodhouse remarks:

> The congregation was the school of democracy. There the humblest member might hear, and join in the debate, might witness the discovery of the natural leader, and participate in that curious process by which there emerges from the clash of many minds a vision clearer and a determination wiser than any single mind could achieve. . . . If the Leveller [radical Puritan] emphasizes the contract on which the authority of just government depends, and insists on the principle of consent, he has had, in his church, experience of a community organized on these very principles. (Woodhouse, *Puritans and Liberty*, p. 76)

The Fulfilling the Promise survey asked, "What are your dreams for the UU movement?" A strong majority of us said our highest hope is to "become a visible and influential force for good in the world."

The history of covenant-making shows that the means for tremendous influence for the common good are in our hands. We do not need more money, although money always helps when we are as liberal regarding money as we are in other matters. We do not need more people, although it would be good to have them, and many in our society need what congregational life can give. To be an influential force for good, what we need to do is establish more strongly in our congregational life the practices that embody loving, just, and sustainable community. We need to be what we want to see, and make visible an alternative to the forms of oppression, alienation, and injustice alive in our time.

Doing so will be a form of keeping faith with the covenant we are already in—the covenant of resistance to oppression. To fail to do so will be to break covenant with those who came before us, who built the house we gratefully inhabit.

Though the path be hard and long,
Still we strive in expectation;

Join we now their ageless song
One with them in aspiration.
One in name, in honor one,
Guard we well the crown they won:
What they dreamed be ours to do,
Hope their hopes and seal them true.

It is exciting to contemplate what might be asked of us, and what promise we might fulfill, if we took this task with seriousness and gave our lives to it.

But it will take courage to do this. It will take spiritual stamina and strength. To find it, we will have to go by a path that we may not want to follow. We will have to look at the complicity of our religious tradition in the failure of our society to be just and sustainable.

BROKEN COVENANT AND BEYOND

The history of covenant-making shows us that covenants can fail, can be broken, or can be severely compromised. In our time, the broken covenant we live in is loss of love for neighbor and care for the earth. The dismantling of welfare, the increasing gap between rich and poor, the marginalization of the most disadvantaged, and the abuse of the environment are profound social failures. This broken covenant has come about through economic practices unsuccessfully checked by values beyond individual gain. The covenantal tradition that we claim as our own has tragically helped to bring this about. We are implicated in the deep intertwining of radical individualism and economic self-interest. Robert Bellah named this for us on Saturday night:

> Almost from the beginning the sacredness of conscience of the individual person was linked to the right to pursue one's own economic interests . . . freedom of conscience and freedom of enterprise are more closely, even genealogically, linked than many of us would like to believe. . . . It is not accident, as they say, that the United States, with its high evaluation of the individual person, is nonetheless alone among North Atlantic societies in the percentage of our population who live in poverty and that we are dismantling what was already the weakest welfare state of any North Atlantic nation. . . . And this is in not small part due to the fact that

our religious individualism is linked to an economic individualism which . . . ultimately knows nothing of the sacredness
of the individual.

Naming our dilemma is a start. Feeling it is also important. In this
brokenness, lives are fragmented, the luster of living is lost for all of
us, and we are missing something important. It matters that we not
deny this.

Adrienne Rich provides an image for our situation in her poem,
"Power":

.   .   .   .

Today I was reading about Marie Curie:
she must have known she suffered   from radiation sickness
her body bombarded for years   by the element
she had purified
It seems she denied to the end
the source of the cataracts on her eyes
the cracked and suppurating skin   of her finger-ends
till she could no longer hold   a test-tube or a pencil

She died   a famous woman   denying
her wounds
denying
her wounds   came   from the same source as her power

(from *Dream of a Common Language*)

How will we find the spiritual resource to purify our souls? What
will it take for us to untangle our deepest religious value—the
sacredness of the individual and the importance of freedom—from
its alliance with an economic system that is failing the poor and
threatening the earth? What must we do to find a new heart, unfet-
tered by the false alliance of freedom with greed?

A final story from the history of covenantal theology provides
some clues to a way ahead. The first great failure of Puritan
covenantal life occurred in 1649 in England. The Puritans had led a
movement to reform English society, to end abuses of power by the
monarch, to advocate for land reform, prison reform, alleviation of
poverty, unjust laws, burdensome taxes, debtors prisons, and so

forth. Fueled by the power of covenant-making and the principles of free conscience, free speech, open debate and dissent, they rode a tide of high hope and put their love of freedom and their opposition to oppression into dramatic action.

In 1649 they won. King Charles was deposed and Cromwell came to power. But as soon as he was in power, in order to make a stronger alliance with those in England interested in economic expansion, Cromwell moved to suppress the radical Puritans who had helped bring him into power. Two groups of Cromwell's supporter were crushed. The Levellers, Puritans with a passion for reform, and the Diggers, even more radical advocates of economic change, were imprisoned, silenced, punished.

The broken-hearted visionaries protested, implored, appealed, demanded that the covenental commitments be honored, but they were squelched. In the aftermath of that broken covenant, more Separatists came to America hoping that a new land would provide greater hope.

In England, new religious movements emerged. One was called the Ranters. The Ranters responded to the anguish of a broken covenant in an outbreak of rage. Quaker scholar Douglas Gywn describes them this way:

> . . . like the unemployed ranks of punks in England of the 1970s snarling "no future," the Ranters were a disturbed and disturbing presence within a receding utopian horizon. In an era of intense covenant theology, their ranting oath-swearing was the perfect expression of rage, a dissonant diatribe that flung covenantal blasphemies aimlessly in all directions. Ranters frightened the Church, the Government, and almost everyone else. (Douglas Gywn, *The Covenant Crucified: Quakers and the Rise of Capitalism*)

The Ranters evolved a nihilistic theology that paired light and darkness as one, and viewed good and evil as intertwined. When put in prison, they quickly recanted. Brokenhearted, they held to no principles that were worth living or dying for.

Another group to emerge was called the Seekers. Douglas Gwyn, again:

> [The Seekers were] individuals who passed from one new group to the next, finally coming together in the twilight of

radicalism, united in their sense of what they had *not* found.
The Seekers saw that none of the current agendas was adequate to the situation . . . they met in silence . . . they awaited
a new revelation from God . . . to plumb these mystifying
depths. . . . Rather than lapse into nihilistic rage, they settled
into a penitent silence that kept the covenant faith even
beyond human understanding. . . . A renewed emphasis was
placed upon the overwhelming power of God's grace and the
need for human stillness to sense the spirit's motions. . . .
They watched and waited in the dark night of eclipse.

In despair at the suppression of the radical Puritans, the Seekers
literally became wanderers. One of the wanderers was George Fox,
who was a youth when Cromwell turned on his co-religionists and
dashed their hopes. Fox left home and traveled from village to village asking the Puritan clergy if they could answer him in his suicidal despair. He sought refuge in nature: sleeping in open fields and
in trees in the forest. For ten years he wandered, and in his wander-
ing a new religious awareness came to him.

Through desolation, the despair of broken covenant, he began to
experience the presence of a spirit of life, sustaining him and all of
life. He articulated this spiritual discovery with these words:
"Inward life did spring up in me." From this spiritual discovery he
formulated, in Gwyn's description, "a deeper spiritual practice . . . a
tender pacifism melded to a fierce commitment to social activism
fueled by a sense of hope born through trial."

Among us there is a deep spiritual longing. According to the
Fulfilling the Promise survey, over 75 percent of us feel something is
missing in Unitarian Universalism. And when asked to identify
what is missing, we said "spiritual discipline and depth."

We need to see the longing for spirituality among us as an expression of our awareness of broken covenant—of something that is failing in our culture, a promise unfulfilled. All of us who have come
into Unitarian Universalism from another religious context know
something of promises broken. All of us as human beings have experienced promises not kept. We know the impasse and the anguish
that comes to human life when commitments are broken.

We need to see our own longing for a deeper and more disciplined spiritual life as a sign that we are aware that something is
missing. It is by patient pursuit of this longing, including the will-

ingness to wander without its anguish being relieved, that fresh vision will come. The place of limit becomes the place of revelation. Gywn writes of the spiritual renewal of the Quakers:

> To arrive there, they had passed through a desolating fire of disillusionment, despair, and purification. This spirituality of desolation not only transformed their inward life; it also radicalized their social vision. The new religious consciousness was a true eruption from the political unconsciousness, a disturbing upwelling of the otherwise repressed "knowledge from below."

The path to deeper spirituality begins in the experience of promises failed, covenant broken, hope suppressed. It begins with disillusionment, impasse, and grief. And it passes through the fire to a new revelation. This is the path we need to follow to find a new heart.

In our time, seekers wander from church to church asking, "Can you answer my despair?" Ranters cry out in the public square, their anguish filling public space with the witness of our collective breach of faith. We suppress either of them at our peril—either within ourselves or around us. For each is part of the path from broken covenant, failure, and limit to a fresh discovery of the deeper resources for hope and strength. From that discovery arises new practices, new covenant. From there is found a center of religious illumination strong enough to move us beyond the limits of our inheritance into fresh hope and creativity.

We must never tire of asking the question that the rich young ruler put to Jesus: "Who is my neighbor?" And we must never abandon the path Guatama followed. Seeing, as he did, who our neighbor is and what the condition of their life and therefore our life is, we must seek and continue to seek, until in whatever forest we find the illumination in our time. It came to George Fox in the wilderness of seeking, and to many forbears in the faith, in the community of resistance: There is a Universal love of which we are a part. There is something that will not let us go. It is in obedience to this truth that the promise of life is fulfilled in us and we become a blessing to the world.

Whether we know, as I've heard theologian Bill Jones describe, "a fierce rebellion lodged in the human heart that will rage against oppression and injustice and fight it to the end out of sheer cantankerousness of spirit, with nothing to sustain it beyond passionate determination" or know it with the tenderness, as I know it, of one who has passed through the valley of suicidal despair. There is a divine comforter who has never left and will never leave and who embraces even the violators of every covenant within the fire of redeeming love. The experience of brokenness becomes the place of revelation; and that revelation is what will fuel a new covenant.

The finding of a deeper center is often through the fire of broken hearts. It is the Seeker and the Ranter in us and around us that can lead us into the future. Stillness that listens and Rage that protests will guide us to a new covenant if we have the courage to refuse to flee from our tears and embody what we come to know in everyday practices.

So, given the lessons of history, let us consider this as a possible expression of our covenant:

> Let us covenant with one another
> > to keep faith with the source of life
> > knowing that we are not our own,
> > earth made us.
> Let us covenant with one another
> > to keep faith with the community of resistance
> > never to forget that life can be saved
> > from that which threatens it
> > by even small bands of people
> > choosing to put into practice
> > an alternative way of life.
> And, let us covenant with one another
> > to seek for an ever deeper awareness
> > of that which springs up inwardly in us.
> > Even when our hearts are broken
> > by our own failure
> > or the failure of others
> > cutting into our lives,
> > Even when we have done all we can
> > and life is still broken,
> > there is a Universal Love
> > that has never broken faith with us
> > and never will.

This is the ground of our hope,
  and the reason we can be bold in seeking to fulfill the
  promise.

QUESTIONS FOR DISCUSSION

1. Parker states that "we receive who we are before we choose who
   we will become." What does she mean by this? What implications does it have for covenant making?

2. Parker points out that "The free church tradition emerged in the
   . . . sixteenth . . . century as part of a reforming movement. . . ."
   What elements of this tradition are as relevant today as they
   were then?

3. Parker asks the question, "What will it take for us to untangle
   our deepest religious value—the sacredness of the individual
   and of freedom—from alliance with an economic system that
   fails the poor and threatens the earth?" Do you agree this is our
   deepest religious value? Why is covenanting a potentially effective response to the problem?

The Covenant of Spiritual Freedom

George Kimmich Beach

Editor's Note. George Kimmich Beach suggests that freedom from shared obligations—doing your own thing—is transient in liberal religion. What is permanent is the idea of spiritual freedom—the human capacity to act with creative goodwill, to perform good works in any situation, however dire. The author calls on us to covenant in spiritual freedom for a new humanity. Beach received his S.T.B. and TH.M. from Harvard Divinity School and a D.Min. from Wesley Theological Seminary. He was senior minister of the Unitarian Universalist Church of Arlington, Virginia, for eighteen years. He is a member of the UUA Commission on Appraisal. Beach is the author of If Yes Is the Answer, What Is the Question? *(Skinner House Books, 1995), and has edited three books of essays by James Luther Adams. This essay is reprinted from* The Transient and Permanent in Liberal Religion *(Skinner House Books, 1995).*

The twentieth century is the age of the crisis of liberal democracy. The prospect of our liberal faith is intimately bound up with that crisis. We face this one question in many guises: Is freedom the right of individuals to think and to do as they please, or is it the human capacity to respond creatively to the possibilities and limits of human existence?

The idea was planted in the eighteenth century, and flourished in the nineteenth century, that people could come together and govern themselves intelligently, virtuously, and with goodwill. Given liberty, they would recognize each other's "inalienable rights," exercise their individual franchise, and form majority governments. Democratic governments would respect the rights of the minority. These ideals seemed self-evident, and the human prospect seemed bright with promise. Jefferson called participation in the affairs of the common weal "the public happiness." Troubling questions of slavery and racism were bypassed by all but a few.

Today's Unitarianism and Universalism were born in this bold "Age of Enlightenment," and nursed on its cultural and political ideals. "I am always young for liberty," declared William Ellery Channing. Cradled in the early years of the American republic, we grew to vigorous young adulthood in the nineteenth century, an era of expanding confidence in the human destiny. Earlier generations spoke of faith in divine Providence; James Freeman Clarke announced Unitarian faith in "the progress of mankind, onward and upward forever."

Today, however, we are reticent about "progress" and wary of rationalistic answers to the deep, emotion-laden issues of psyche and society. For instance, when we hear Ralph Waldo Emerson's words, "Whoso would be a man must be a nonconformist," we may as well think of loners or arrogant "self-made men" as we do of self-reliant individualists. Today we see rugged individualism is the problem, not the answer. These are symptoms of how far we have traveled into liberalism's age of crisis. Our nineteenth-century forebears called theirs "the great century." Raymond Aron called the twentieth, "the century of total war"—for now whole populations take up arms against each other. W. H. Auden called our age "the age of anxiety."

The twenty-first century will bring a new social context and, in consequence, a new meaning of "freedom": sharper awareness of the human limits and a narrowed sense of human possibilities. Does this mean an end of personal and social freedom as we know it? As an ideology of individualism, yes; as a socially embodied spiritual reality, no. Abraham Lincoln called for "a new birth of freedom" in the crisis of his age; we must call for a new covenant of freedom in the crisis of our age.

We Unitarian Universalists remain the children of the age of reason and democracy, of science-driven human progress and the discovery of human rights. We remain, also, the heirs of a noble tradition of liberal concern for civic values, social justice, and peace. This secular heritage is rooted in a theological affirmation: the dignity and sanctity of every person as a bearer of the image of God.

A fundamental re-formation of the human Spirit is emerging in our time. We must understand ourselves as engaged in that historic mission. We must believe that history is the story of freedom, agonized by the global struggle for justice. Or else our salt has lost its savor and may as well be cast out.

We too easily wrap ourselves in the cocoon of our own congregational life and forget that we are part of a world-historical movement. We dwindle into coziness and forget what brought us together in the first place: the keen sense that what we want most is to be part of something great—a historical drama in which we are actors and everything we cherish is at stake.

Birthright anti-traditionalists though we be, we are the bearers of a cherished tradition: liberalism has been the costing commitment of many before us. We believe in ourselves, but we are not sectarians who believe only in "we few." We affirm our congregations as agents of the church universal, the covenant people.

We are a covenant people, a spiritual community that is found wherever people come together in faithfulness to values that sustain and renew the common life of the public world. We must be explicit about what those values are. They are expressed in every age and tradition; the prophets of ancient Israel announced them in ringing tones: justice, faithfulness, steadfast love, mercy, truthfulness, goodwill, and peace.

These prophetic, covenantal values constitute us as a people. We did not choose them; by eliciting our commitment, they "choose" us. They are not optional ("preferences"), but essential to (creators of) our being. The covenant people is found everywhere around the globe and in all ages. It comes into being wherever people form communities dedicated to sustaining and renewing this vision—whenever they say, "This is the very meaning of our life together."

Transient is the reduction of "freedom" to "personal preference" and "do your own thing." Transient is the confusion of "liberal" with "lax," an ideology of freedom from shared obligations. Transient is the liberal church that is no more than a refuge from "orthodoxy," no more than a club for "our kind of people," a monoculture of the like-minded.

Permanent in liberal religion is this: devotion to spiritual freedom, the human capacity to act with creative goodwill in any situation, however dire. Freedom is a miracle, something inexplicable. It is demonstrated in our capacity to surpass ourselves. It is a spiritual reality that enables us to create a new thing under the sun, when we fulfill its conditions, its covenant.

What are the conditions—the requirements—of this covenant? Micah asks, "What does Yahweh require of you?" and he answers in terms of the prophetic, covenantal values: "to do justly, to love kind-

ness, and to walk humbly with your God." Freedom is not free for
the taking. We have it on exacting conditions: that we remember our
finitude, our frailty, our fallibility—and therefore our interdependence. That we remember that we have personhood only in community (or we'd have died in infancy) and community only with commitment (or we won't have it for long). That we remember that liberation begins with ourselves, for it means freeing ourselves from
whatever stands between us and the divine image—the creative
goodwill—in which we are made. That we remember the principle
of humility: "This I cannot do alone, nor for myself alone, but only
with your help, by the grace of God." That we live within a sacred
covenant, and when we have broken it, we can renew it, in faith that
this too is the promise of "the love that will not let us go."

Having made spiritual freedom central, our difficulties with
"freedom"—reducing it to a manageable and appealing ideology—
are almost inevitable. We are no exception to the general rule: What
is celebrated as central in every religion is what gives it the most
trouble. For instance, Jews rejoiced in being the chosen for Yahweh's
covenant, and what it got them was Yahweh's denunciation, in
Amos's prophetic interpretation: "You only have I known of all the
families of the earth; therefore I will punish you for all your iniqui-
ties." (Amos 3:2) Our brave new covenants are forever degenerating
into contracts—manageable "deals." Prophets, then, will arise, calling us to rediscover the miracle of freedom and renew the covenant
of spiritual freedom.

Every religion worth its salt is founded on a miracle. This may
seem disconcerting in a church that has made a specialty out of
denying the existence of miracles. By reducing "miracle" to something contrary to science and reason—rather than the reality of spiritual liberation given through divine grace, clothed in ancient
story—we denude the imagination. We become incomprehensible
even to ourselves.

We are not free to believe whatever we want, any more than we
are free to do whatever we want—unless, of course, we choose
instant gratification and utter transience. We are free to believe what
we must and to do what we must, in order to fulfill our human voca-
tion, our calling to a larger humanity. The phrase, "in order that,"
signals an often-forgotten truth: freedom is only meaningful within
a framework of purposeful action. The word *covenant* signifies a

framework within which intentionality takes effect. Spiritual freedom seeks authentic self-transcendence. Within this framework we enjoy much latitude for individual expression. Our religious communities should enjoy a diversity as various as humanity itself. But the convenantal framework itself is not optional; it is necessary, fated, and inescapable: "That's the deal," as Joy Gresham said to C. S. Lewis. We stumble over this truth again and again: Human possibilities emerge and shine most brightly in the face of limitations.

In other words, freedom emerges against a background of necessity, like a meteor in the night sky. Nicholas of Cusa spoke of "the coincidence of opposites"; freedom and necessity seem to be near opposites that nearly coincide. In time and history they are dialectically related, polarities of the kind Plato had in mind when he spoke of the one and the many, "one form pervading a scattered multitude, and many different forms contained under one higher form." (Sophist 253d)

This abstract matter can be made concrete by considering the process of creating pottery on a wheel. When as a potter you form a lump of clay, you make many decisions, exercising your freedom both consciously and instinctively, to one end, a finished ceramic. The first step is highly self-conscious: "What do I want to make? Well, the possibilities are infinite—within the limits of the material, the tools, and my skill. Still, these limits are not absolute: I might venture a wholly new form, and succeed!"

The original decision in pottery making is not unlike the original decision of faith: once a direction has been set, soon it will be too late to change your mind. Choosing a bowl excludes a pitcher. Now choices are being made within an ever-narrowing range; necessity is closing in on the maker. But this is the miracle of creation: a reversal is also in progress, for the embrace of necessity gives birth to a greater freedom. With each choice, new, more refined choices arise; creative freedom is growing exponentially.

As in pottery making, so too in life: the process of making is also a process of discovering, for as the form takes shape, it begins to gain a life and an integrity of its own. As our gross, material freedom is narrowed, mirabile dictu our refined, spiritual freedom grows by leaps and bounds. Suddenly we remember Nicholas of Cusa's principle: opposites coincide. The perfect end to the exercise of freedom is perfect necessity. We think: This bowl, or this life, can only be what it must be!

Do we romanticize the creative artist in us to say so? No doubt we do, but we think it anyway: Intentionality and practice conspire together to produce what is inevitable, "just so," complete and perfect. Although it never quite turns out that way—although the result is, by turns, both humbling and exalting—still, the miracle of having a hand in making a new thing has occurred. Spiritual freedom is like that: it exalts and humbles us again and again.

James Luther Adams said, in *The Prophethood of All Believers*, "I call that church free which in covenant with the divine community-forming power brings the individual, even the unacceptable, into a caring, trusting fellowship that protects and nourishes integrity and spiritual freedom. Its goal is the prophethood and the priesthood of all believers—the one for the liberty of prophesying, the other for the ministry of healing."

Adams wrote these words for the 1975 sesquicentennial celebration of the American Unitarian Association, founded in 1825. They echo Channing's famous lines on the theme, "I call that mind free," from his Election Sermon of 1830, titled "Spiritual Freedom." But where Channing's heroic individualism exalted "the free mind," Adams's chastened liberalism, having imbibed the political and cultural crises of the twentieth century, exalts "the church that is free."

Between Channing and Adams there is both a continuity and radical break: both speak of spiritual freedom, but with Adams, no longer the individual but "the dedicated community" (Paul Weiss) is the matrix, the sacred birthplace, of freedom. The dedicated community itself is the liberating reality, and our task as a liberal church is to model that for the world.

This accent also marks a renewal of theological awareness, for beyond the social vision lies a cosmic and sacred vision: "the interdependent web of existence of which we are a part." Jim Adams named it "the covenant of being." This is an unaccustomed way of thinking, for us, and it will provoke resistance. Nevertheless, this paradigm shift will transform our free faith in the new millennium, rescuing our permanency, the covenant of spiritual freedom, from our transience, the church as way station en route to the golf course.

We covenant in spiritual freedom for a new humanity. *We covenant:* We freely commit ourselves to high and holy aims, aims that transcend us, aims of the Spirit. Not in freedom from obligations to others, but in freedom to enter into common endeavors for the common good. Not in freedom from the nourishing roots of our faith in ancient ages, but in freedom to give fresh interpretation to ancient symbols and stories. Not in freedom from being called to aims that surpass us, but in the freedom that springs from knowing that "we've caught a moving train" (Johnny Ray Youngblood), and, together, we're on our way.

We covenant in spiritual freedom. We find at the center of our faith an energizing mainspring, a drive for meaning and dignity implanted in every soul in every land—the wonder of being alive and awakened to life, the grace of beginning anew. Not in the self-enclosing isolation of the self, but in the quest for a more inclusive covenant. Not in narrow-mindedness or in mean-spirited debunking of things cherished by others, but in listening for the spirit of life and truth wherever it arises. Not in fearfulness that life runs out and nothing can be done, but in the courage to turn every crisis of life into an opportunity for growth and spiritual depth.

We covenant in spiritual freedom for a new humanity. We seek a better world where all peoples can flourish, sharing in the resources of planet Earth and sustaining her natural ecology, a new humanity within the covenant of being. Not closing our eyes to the awesome tasks that stand before us, but committing ourselves to labor tirelessly for the physical, moral, and spiritual well-being of all. Not despairing of the human prospect, but affirming hope, and the sacredness of the image in which we are made. Not stonyhearted when we are called to make a new beginning, nor giving up when our need is to persevere, but affirming our quest for wholeness and holiness.

Questions for Discussion

1. George Kimmich Beach suggests that the history of Unitarianism and Universalism is deeply connected with the rise of democracy in the modern age, and that its current dilemmas are bound up with "the crisis of liberal democracy" in our time. What does this mean? Do you agree?

2. How does Beach suggest that the meaning of "freedom" needs to be transformed? What is the difference between political free-

dom and spiritual freedom? How is this related to the "negative" and the "positive" ideas of freedom?

3. Beach writes: "We are a covenant people, a spiritual community that is found wherever people come together in faithfulness to values that sustain and renew the common life of the public world." Do you agree that is what we are? He continues: "We must be explicit about what those values are." What are they? What validates them?

4. In regard to the ideas of the nature of human freedom, what is the continuity, and what is the discontinuity, between the visions of William Ellery Channing and James Luther Adams? Do you agree with Beach's assertion about "the permanent in liberal religion," namely the sentence explicated in the last three paragraphs: "We covenant in spiritual freedom for a new humanity"?

The Eternal Yes

Walter P. Herz

Editor's Note. I originally presented the following essay as a lay sermon for my own congregation, the First Unitarian Church of Cincinnati in an attempt to create a compelling rationale for covenanting in contemporary liberal religion. I conclude with a proposed covenant. A somewhat truncated version of this essay appeared in the UU Voice. *I have revised it for this book.*

During the 1995 General Assembly debate amending our Unitarian Universalist Association (UUA) Bylaws, I experienced an epiphany. While listening to the heated discussion over adding yet one more to our already lengthy list of sources in the statement of our Principles and Purposes, my long-standing vague sense of dissatisfaction with the fuzziness of Unitarian Universalism resolved into sharp focus. I saw clearly that we Unitarians, in our flight from our roots, trying to become ever more inclusive, have stretched the concept of a religious association beyond clear meaning. In appealing abstractly to so wide a range of theological positions, we have ended with a UUA covenant so wordy and diffuse it evokes minimal spiritual response. Our meaning is inordinately difficult to communicate readily to the uninitiated. Moreover, members of our congregations are sadly lacking in consciousness that we are responsible for stewardship of Unitarian Universalist heritage, faith, and institutional vigor. Our failure of stewardship—and by stewardship I mean an active commitment to the preservation and growth of congregations living our values—has severely limited the expansion and impact of liberal religion and jeopardizes our future.

I make a strong charge. It's *not* a new charge. New is a growing recognition among us that contemporary Unitarian Universalists need a greater sense of shared devotion we can all celebrate in the context of a religious institution. Only this will summon stewardship among our members and congregations as the norm, and effect the resurrection of liberal religion as a spiritual home and a social force. I will first sketch the historical reasons for our present situation. Then I will suggest how we might nurture and bring to fruition an Easter event among us.

Our American Unitarian roots reach back to the English Separatists who settled New England. A small number of believers known as the Pilgrims separated from the Church of England because they believed individuals in the congregation possessed rightful and holy power to practice and to share their own religious teachings and observances. A much larger number of Puritans—extremists aiming to remove all traces of Romanism from the English Church—emigrated to model and to practice their understanding of the purified church out of the reach of the Church of England. Both groups adopted congregational polity by which they meant each congregation's rule by the Holy Spirit as known and experienced in the local body without hierarchical rule by bishops. During the seventeenth and eighteenth centuries these Congregationalists gradually divided into a liberal wing (including the Pilgrim Church) whose members believed in a more rational and individual approach to seeking religious truth, and a conservative wing focused more on the fallen sinner's need for repentance. The two wings had begun to separate during the 1780s by which time numerous liberal ministers were questioning the dogma of the Trinity. By 1805, when Harvard chose a Unitarian as professor of divinity over an old-line Puritan candidate, the split was all but complete. William Ellery Channing gave his landmark sermon on Unitarian Christianity in 1819. But by then 100 or so Congregational churches in New England had long since become Unitarian. Most kept their Congregational label a while longer. All remained fervently committed to congregational polity, the doctrine of local authority in all matters of faith and practice.

In the 1830s Transcendentalism burst onto the scene with its emphasis on intuition, emotion, and direct personal communion with the divine without reference to any social or historical developments or institutions. Channing had proclaimed "man's likeness to God." Emerson declared, "I am part or parcel of God." Transcendentalists preached that God is everywhere, in all creation, especially in each human. Theodore Parker carried this to its logical conclusion when he proclaimed that Christianity could exist separately from Christ in the form of pure morality as known to the individual conscience, "for Christianity is not a system of doctrines, but rather a method of attaining oneness with God," which demands living an ethical life. Conrad Wright termed Parker's doctrine "the ultimate logic of religious individualism." It is significant that although Parker was without doubt the most famous and most influential preacher/writer of his generation, his congregation did not survive his death. The transcendentalist leaders were not institutionalists.

By the time of the Civil War Unitarianism was in turmoil, the chasm widening between the traditionalist Christian Unitarians and the radical Transcendentalist/Parkerites who were in the process of shedding any remaining vestiges of shared tradition. The American Unitarian Association, founded in 1825 for missionary purposes, had lost much of its funding. Henry Bellows, a prominent New York minister, recognized that Unitarians had to organize more effectively on a national basis or dwindle and die. Under his leadership a convention was held in New York in April 1865. Three quarters of the Unitarian churches were represented by ministers and lay leaders. Following fierce debate between the traditionalists and radicals, the new National Conference of Unitarian Churches, by an overwhelming majority, adopted this preamble to its constitution:

Whereas the great opportunities and demands for Christian labor and consecration at this time increase our sense of the obligations of all disciples of the Lord Jesus Christ to prove their faith by self-denial and by the devotion of their lives and possessions to the service of God and the building up of the Kingdom of his son, therefore . . .

The next year at the first annual meeting of the National Conference, radicals tried to remove reference to the lordship of Jesus from the preamble. Once again they lost by a wide margin. So the radicals, including many highly promising young ministers, withdrew and founded the Free Religious Association (FRA) in 1867, "its objective being," according to its preamble, "to promote the interest of pure religion, to increase fellowship in the spirit and to encourage the scientific study of man's religious nature and history." Note the abstract terms used to define the objective (purpose) of the FRA.

Gone was any reference to particular social or historical people, individuals, or groups. Everything was completely generalized.

The FRA was made up of approximately 10 percent of all Unitarian ministers; they had left the National Conference. FRA membership included also a number of other religious liberals invited to join, some prominent reform Jewish rabbis, humanists, deists, atheists, and other outspoken opponents of orthodoxy. Even opponents of all religion were accepted. From 1867 to 1894 Unitarian ministers in the FRA participated in endless debates with the National Conference, which voted on numerous peace formulas. In consonance with their historical desire to be inclusive, the traditionalist majority inched ever closer to the position of the minority radicals. Finally, in September 1894 in Saratoga, New York, the National Conference unanimously adopted this new preamble.

> These churches accept the religion of Jesus, holding, in accordance with his teaching, that practical religion is summed up in love to God and love to man. The Conference recognizes the fact that its constituency is Congregational in tradition and polity. Therefore, it declares that nothing in this constitution is to be construed as an authoritative test; and we cordially invite to our working fellowship any who, while differing from us in belief, are in general sympathy with our spirit and our practical aims.

One factor remained constant, however, as it had from our beginnings, an uncompromising commitment to congregational polity. New was a vastly wider spectrum of theological positions from traditional Christian Unitarian to atheism. We had taken on an unprecedented pluralism.

And so we are pluralistic today, more than a century later, with approximately 150,000 adult members—about the same number reported at merger thirty-five years ago (although the older number was undoubtedly overstated). Congregational polity and an extraordinarily diffuse range of theological preferences reign. If one accepts the necessity of liberal religion's expansion in numbers and influence as a given—and I most emphatically do—the question to which we must find a viable answer is this: How can we achieve a more effective association while still maintaining the essential core values of congregational polity and without compromising the obligation and freedom of each member to hold his/her own personal theology?

I believe that creation of a new and widely affirmed covenant is the sine qua non of our resurrection as an effective religious institution. In the following discussion I have adopted Forrester Church's definition: "Religion is our human response to the dual reality of being alive and having to die. All religious beliefs and the actions stemming from them reflect an attempt, human and therefore imperfect, to make sense of life and death by finding meaning in both."

I followed three guidelines in developing a new covenant. First, I believe it is essential to use the traditional religious vocabulary. I agree with John Buehrens, our UUA president, who said, "We religious liberals haven't merely shot ourselves in the foot by abandoning all the most powerful language and imagery of our culture. We have shot ourselves in the mouth, where it's fatal. Talk about wings! We have turned over such language to the right wing. And they have flown with it." Our efforts to communicate with the culture at large are a failure because people do not find our language authentic. We must use the common religious vocabulary—*with our own liberal* religious meanings.

Second, I believe strongly that our covenant needs to be suffused with the Universalist spirit. I have thus far spoken overwhelmingly of our Unitarian ancestors. They were highly articulate, urban, and college educated. Unitarian leaders overshadowed the more rural Universalists, and Unitarian members outnumbered Universalists three to one at the time of our merger. However, Unitarians in the nineteenth century were too much concerned with what they were denying. The then more numerous and upbeat Universalists proclaimed an easily understood, optimistic message exemplifying the "eternal Yes" Frederic Henry Hedge demanded when he said, "Enough of negation! Enough of destruction! Enough of rationalism! Have done with denying; the soul demands something positive. Give us the everlasting Yes!"[1] In his excellent book, *If Yes is the Answer, What is the Question?*, George Kimmich Beach quotes this meditation by Jacob Trapp.

The most important word in our language is yes.
It matters what we say yes to.
It matters what we say no to.

Every no gets its value from the yes it also affirms
To say no to what denies and destroys is also to say yes to what
    affirms, builds, creates.
God, said Nathan Söderblom, is the everlasting yes of existence.
(Nathan Söderblom was an early twentieth-century Swedish
Lutheran theologian.)

Third, I suggest we use what I call a metonymic approach to
developing our covenant. Those familiar with rhetoric know that
metonymy is the use of a suggestive word for what is meant, or the
substitution of a symbol for the thing itself. I will use traditional religious vocabulary in a metonymic sense, with each UU having the
responsibility of supplying his or her own meanings, thereby defining his or her personal theological position.

Here I review the three subjects of a covenant I regard as essential. James Luther Adams, the greatest Unitarian theologian of the
twentieth century, in his essay, "A Faith for the Free," lists three liberal religious tenets:

1. Our ultimate dependence for being and freedom is upon a creative power and upon processes not of our own making.

2. The commanding, sustaining, transforming reality finds its
richest focus in meaningful human history, in free, cooperative effort
for the common good.

3. The achievement of freedom in community requires the power
of organization and the organization of power.

In *Myths of Time and History*, Alice Blair Wesley names the subjects
of a covenant suggested by these tenets as the nature of God, the
nature of humanity, and the nature of the church. Insofar as God is
concerned, it's incomprehensible to me that countless religious liberals still shy away from grappling with the symbol in a positive
way. After all, the notion of God as a bearded white male enthroned
in heaven somewhere up there is long since passé in all but the most
fundamentalist circles, and probably in many of those too! The
meaning of God has been divested of anthropomorphism and
degendered by theologians and is, as often as not, described as a
human construct. For example, Paul Tillich wrote that "God is symbol of God." Gordon Kaufman stated that "the image/concept 'God'
is a human constructed symbol." Bernard Loomer wrote that "the
term 'God' is the symbol of ultimate values and meanings." I also

like Forrester Church's description of what concerns him ultimately: "God is our name for the mystery that wells within and looms beyond the limits of our being. Life force, spirit of life, ground of being, these too are names for the unnameable which I am now content to call my God." Atheism, a frequently held position, is a well-accepted concept among Unitarian Universalists. However, theologians seem generally to agree that only the small minority of those who truly have no concern over the meaning of existence, who are totally indifferent toward the ultimate question, really qualify as atheists. Tillich wrote, "He who denies God as a matter of ultimate concern affirms God because he affirms ultimacy in his concern." I have concluded that the only thing we liberal religionists have to fear in using the term *God* is fear itself, a fear of how the orthodox may have defined it, or a fear of what other Unitarian Universalists might think of us. I harbored this fear for well over thirty years as a Unitarian Universalist until I finally recognized God's value—even necessity—as a symbol in liberal religion.

The second subject of a covenant, the nature of humanity, is concerned with how we live our lives, what ways work for health and holiness, or, to use a good Biblical word, salvation. I regard as fundamental the so-called Golden Rule, Love thy neighbor as thyself. Expressed in Leviticus 19 and later in Matthew 22 and Mark 12, it was formulated in similar words by Rabbis Hillel and Akiba, by the charismatic holy man and healer Hanina ben Dosa, a younger contemporary of Jesus, by Confucius in the fifth century BCE, by Mohammed in the Hadith, and by Immanuel Kant as his Categorical Imperative. I also find crucial the understanding expressed in the epistle of James that "faith without works is dead." Paul and Luther taught that salvation comes by faith alone. Luther so disliked James's epistle that he would have discarded it from the Bible if he could have. James's emphasis on the practice of good works was a concept so treasured by the Universalists that they included it in their confessions of faith in 1803, 1899, and 1935.

The third subject of a covenant, the nature of the church, is about the church's means of acting as a community. A covenant familiar to all that all can honestly affirm will initiate the resurrection of our religious institution, empowering us with strength to ensure the preservation and growth of our heritage without compromising congregational polity or the obligation in freedom of each individual to hold his or her own theological interpretation.

Following is my suggested new covenant followed by a reiteration of the first sentence with my own interpolated explanations of what the key words mean *to me*.

Because God infuses each human being with the potential for an ethical and loving life redeemed by performing good works,[2]
We covenant to be a democratic and faithful community welcoming others in their full diversity and providing a religious environment that nurtures and supports each of us in our lifelong efforts to fulfill this potential in our own lives; in the lives of our families, our congregation, and our Unitarian Universalist Association; in the affairs of the larger community; and in our shared stewardship of the natural universe.
Each party to this covenant shall assume the continuing responsibility of interpreting its key words and phrases, thereby maintaining his or her own individual theological position.

And now just the first phrase with my meanings interpolated:

Because God—*the universal life force*—infuses each human being with the potential for an ethical and loving life–as *enunciated by Moses, Jesus and prophetic teachers of many other traditions in the never ending process of revelation*—that is redeemed—*saved from meaninglessness*—by performing good works,

So, there it is, my own personal spiritual statement in a simple metonymic form into which each individual—from the Christian Unitarian Universalist to the atheist still concerned with ultimate meaning—can interpolate his or her own theological position. It *could* suffuse our members and congregations with the spirit of stewardship; it *could* resurrect Unitarian Universalism as a religious association, much as our country's metonymic Constitution created a mighty nation out of a widely disparate population that was insistent on individual rights and thirteen colonies that adamantly maintained their belief in state polity.[3]

E pluribus unum!

NOTES

1. From "The Eternal Yes," Address to the graduating class of Harvard Divinity School, July 15, 1849, by Frederic Henry Hedge.
2. Because some Unitarian Universalists would find it impossible to use the word *God* in a covenant, I suggest as an alternative beginning, "Because each human being is infused with . . ." Then the nature of the infusing agent—be it God, the universal life force, or any of the other countless possibilities—becomes the variable supplied mentally by each individual.
3. While this covenant was originally proposed to one church for its consideration, the approach is equally applicable to the development of a covenant for our association of congregations. Indeed, shouldn't our association's covenant be consistent with those of its member congregations?

Questions for Discussion

1. Herz asserts that there is "a growing recognition among us that contemporary Unitarian Universalists desperately need a greater sense of shared devotion we can all celebrate in the context of a religious institution." What does he mean? Do you agree?

2. Herz encapsules Unitarian history from the liberal ("Arminian" or free will) Puritans through Transcendentalism and the Free Religious Association to the present. What surprises you about the story? Is it a story of progress or dissolution, or in some sense both? How do you feel about the fact that we have approximately the same number of Unitarian Universalists today as we had at merger in 1961?

3. Herz asserts that "creation of a new and widely affirmed covenant is the sine qua non of our resurrection as an effective religious institution." He goes on to specify three criteria for a new covenant: a religious vocabulary, an affirmative spirit, a metonymy. What does he mean by these three criteria?

4. Herz takes the three elements of "a faith for the free" outlined by James Luther Adams and elaborates on them as key terms of the covenant we need. Thus the covenant will speak of (1) the nature of God, (2) the nature of humanity, and (3) the nature of the church. He then ventures his own affirmation, reflecting these categories. Can you write your own covenantal statement of faith? Let's try it, now!

Envoi

Walter P. Herz

Editor's Note. This is the equivalent of a poem's "envoi": a short stanza summarizing its major ideas. In this case, some of my intended readers helped me write it through their discussions with me on the Internet. My thanks to all those who have made participation in our UUA Internet lists such a rewarding experience.

We have seen that liberal religious covenanting is as old as our earliest roots in English Separatism and Puritanism. We have seen also that it is as contemporary as the Commission on Appraisal Report, *Interdependence*, with its potential impact on how we will associate in the new millennium—as individuals within our congregations and as congregations within our association.

Though fundamental to our Unitarian Universalist heritage, covenanting was little discussed in modern liberal religious circles until very recently. In January 1997 the announcement of the UUA Board's recovenanting initiative, Fulfilling the Promise, created some ripples of interest. Then *Interdependence: Renewing Congregational Polity* was introduced at the 1997 General Assembly. It generated active consideration of covenanting as a basic element in our heritage of congregational polity. Further, it stimulated some discussion of its relevance in contemporary Unitarian Universalism.

Many of us have come to realize that theological diversity alone is an entirely inadequate basis for a strongly associated congregation of individuals, or for a truly functional association of congregations. Rather, theological diversity by itself tends to be divisive in the absence of an organizing principle that assures an appropriate behavioral context. It has become increasingly clear that defining and securing agreement on such associational behavior is the critical role of the covenant in liberal religion.

We did not create this book in a vacuum, detached from reality. Following the 1997 General Assembly, a number of Internet chat lines were initiated by the Unitarian Universalist Association (UUA). These were—and are—independent of any UUA authority, and they are refereed by highly competent lay people. Through active participation in a number of these, most particularly the cong-polity, memb-1, and uu-leaders lines, I have been able to get a clear indication of the hunger shared by many Unitarian Universalists for a more definitive process of association along the lines suggested in this book. Excerpts from a few of my Internet conversations will give you a sense of the hunger for association in covenanted relationships.

From a birthright Unitarian Universalist layperson:

I agree with inclusivity, but I disagree with some of the ways we try to achieve it. I suspect that changing the words we use to describe ourselves may serve to include some at the expense of others. For example, I would posit that if one looks at the large numbers of young people joining churches today, we might find that our shying away from traditional "religious" words such as "church" may well be having the unintended effect of keeping many young people away from us. Many young people looking for a religious place to go don't know that a UU Society or Fellowship is what other denominations might call a church, and for that reason alone, they may never consider visiting one of our "churches." This is unintended exclusivity.

I also feel that UUism is so eager to be inclusive that we run the risk of becoming mush. By trying to be all things to all people, we may end up being nothing for anybody. Often, people new to UUism don't like the words used in many UU societies because they bring back memories of the "belief systems" that they left, often with hard feelings. That has always been true, but it seems to me that before we say "Oh, you don't like those words? Well, zap, they're gone!" we need to talk about what these words mean, and can mean, to UUs. Maybe we need to talk seriously about those words, and even hang on to some of them, not for the sake of making anyone uncomfortable or because we simply want to hang onto them, but because they "do" or can have a special and important

meaning for us as UUs. Perhaps more people who come to
UUism should be encouraged to learn about our traditions
and heritage, rather than being encouraged to change that
which they don't like. Perhaps this is a way to be inclusive. . . .

From my response:

I find it difficult to understand why my adherence to the
original organizing principle of liberal religion is taken by
some as opposition to inclusiveness. Quite to the contrary. I
adhere to it because it's the only way I know to make inclusiveness work effectively.

How we behave toward one another locally, toward other
congregations continentally, and toward the interconnected
web universally is what UUism is all about. If we get that
right, theological diversity is very manageable. If we don't
get congregational polity right, we are reduced to an agglomeration of liberal religious boutiques, loosely associated and
without any real organizing principle. In learning about our
heritage one can see the usefulness of traditional religious
vocabulary. Church, congregation, covenant, redemption, etc.
all take on distinctly liberal religious meanings that are very
relevant today. There are entirely too many members of our
congregations to whom UUism remains an escape from religion rather than a haven for religion.

A minister's response:

I think you have spelled out the most difficult and important
of points. How do we help our new members (not to mention
our older members who haven't thought about this much) get
the point that only as we "agree in love" (to quote Ballou, I
believe) can we afford our disagreements and diverse paths.
Without that agreement, no other matters can survive. . . .

The movement arising to develop Congregational
Covenants is, in my mind, a very important step in our
movement. I am sure there will be those who protest that the
covenant is simply another creed. But, so long as we have so
few examples in this society now of mutual commitment and
respectful dialogue (employers, families, schools, neighbor-
hoods, fractured and abandoning the participants), I wonder
if our churches should consider requiring a premembership

"Catechism class" not to teach "what UUs believe" but "how UUs create and remain in covenant—what it means, and what are some of the skills for communication and respectful conflict in a congregation."

~

My posting:

I wonder if Rev. ————'s congregation has agreed on covenant that says how its members promise to act upon the mission statement. It sounds to me as though that may be the missing ingredient.

The minister's response:

I appreciate your comment on my question about the mission statement. You are correct about the "missing ingredient." I am hoping that this church, in the near future, will take a step back and see the necessity for covenant with mission. It will make a great difference. I do still concern myself with Unitarian Universalism's penchant for fads, and hope this very useful part of church work is not just assumed as such.

~

UU lay leader posting:

Dear Fellow Lay Leaders, We just had our annual meeting and were barely able to declare a quorum (35%) at the start of the meeting. The same was true at a special meeting we held earlier this year. By the time we voted on anything, I'm sure we didn't have a quorum in attendance anymore.

I have to admit I find it a little disappointing. . . . I guess I wish determining the future of our church was a higher priority for more of the members. It is an exciting time for us, we are moving toward ministry, and there are lots of decisions to be made, including significant financial ones. But I also know that people are very busy and are doing the best they can.

My response:

I have been nonplused by the acceptance of such low quorum requirements by our congregations, and then by our difficulty in achieving them. I wonder if the two are not related. By this I suppose I'm inferring that our generally low attendance at congregational meetings is a self-fulling prophecy. The question then is why does a faith that prides itself on freedom not exercise that freedom to participate in its governance?

Without going into our heritage in detail, I suggest that this problem is a particularly dramatic example . . . of the fundamental flaw in our practice of liberal religion today. The flaw to which I refer is our lack of understanding of what we are as UUs. Most of our members join without really knowing what they are joining; . . . They have little sense of what congregational polity is all about, i.e., that it is the process of governance that transforms a group of individual searchers with diverse theological beliefs into a congregation that walks together in a loving and supportive relationship.

In other words, low attendance at congregational meetings is a symptom of our denominational malaise, even as difficulties in funding our churches abundantly and in attracting new members are also. To get rid of the symptoms one must attack the basic cause of the condition. Look to ignorance of our heritage with consequent weak covenanting as the cause. Correct it and you'll soon enough see the symptoms disappear. The privilege of self-governance must not be taken lightly in a liberal religious setting. It must be treasured and used well as the expression of our basic religious value—freedom.

Response by the lay leader:

I think a good number of our members have little idea what Unitarian Universalism is beyond finding a bit of inspiration, sanity, and community on Sunday mornings. No idea of the greater organizational structure or congregational polity or conscious concern for our governance of freedom of religion; no sense of mission. Conveying this is a big job.

∽

From a congregation president's posting:

I agree that new members need a stronger sense of just what they are joining, beyond a sense of acceptance and welcome. . . . If we did a better job up front we'd have fewer people leaving. . . . Ignorance of our heritage with consequent weak covenanting are, in my opinion, the very heart of many of the problems I've witnessed. Now here's a question I've asked many times in my congregation: just what is meant by the term covenant?

From my response:

To respond to her question on what is meant by the term "covenant," it is very simply the promises, or agreement, we make with each other regarding how we will behave toward one another in our congregation, in our association of congregations, and toward the interconnected web. Note that it is not a theological statement—it is solely concerned with process. . . . It is this covenant of behavior that makes it possible for a group of people with very diverse theological positions to be a cohesive liberal religious congregation, because they have covenanted to walk together in a loving and supportive relationship.

A minister's response to my posting:

Just want to add amen to your posting on UU leaders. When I switched over from the Methodist ministry thirty-five years ago, I thought the loose structure was great, but now I see the downside. I don't think the solution is imposing requirements from the top (even if that were possible) but in "growing" awareness that joining a UU congregation is a covenental relationship—and if "covenant" doesn't have a theological, it certainly does have a religious meaning.

∼

Covenanting is our quintessential process of creating and nurturing right relationship in association. When we covenant, we recall our past and envision the future so we can redeem the present.

Truly, redeeming time *is* our liberal religious mission—perpetually, day by day and year by year, to the end of time. Let's get on with it!

Questions for Discussion

1. Many of the Internet comments reflect deep discontent with the lack of firm religious consensus about the meaning of Unitarian Universalism and the shallowness of our institutional commitments (both to the local congregation and to the association of congregations). What connection do you see between these two seemingly different things?

2. Explain the title of the book. Do you agree with the Herz's rationale for covenants within congregations?

3. Do you think your congregation should reexamine its vision and its covenantal relationships? How frequently do you believe this should be done?

Bibliography

Adams, James Luther. 1986. *The Prophethood of All Believers.* Ed. George K. Beach. Boston: Beacon Press.

Baldwin, James. 1963. *The Fire Next Time.* New York: Dell.

Bayer, Charles. 1986. *A Guide to Liberation Theology for Middle Class Congregations.* St. Louis: CBP Press.

Beach, George Kimmich. 1995. *If Yes Is the Answer, What Is the Question?* Boston: Skinner House Books.

Bellah, Robert. 1985. *Habits of the Heart: Individualism and Commitment in American Life.* Berkeley: University of California Press.

Berger, Peter, and Thomas Luckman. 1966. *The Social Construction of Reality: A Treatise in the Sociology of Knowledge.* Garden City: Doubleday Anchor.

Buehrens, John. 1993. Roots and wings, in *The Universalist Heritage: Keynote Addresses on Universalist History, Ethics and Theology, 1976–1992.* Syracuse, NY: The New York State Convention of Universalists.

Church, Forrest. 1985. *Father and Son.* New York: Harper & Row.

Gwyn, Douglas. 1990. *The Covenant Crucified: Quakers and the Rise of Capitalism.* Wallingford, CT: Pendle Hill Publishers.

Hacker, Andrew. 1990. Transnational America. *New York Review of Books,* (November 22):19–24.

Kaufman, Gordon. 1993. *In Face of Mystery: A Constructive Theology.* Cambridge: Harvard University Press.

Keen, Sam. 1988. The stories we live by. *Psychology Today,* (December):44.

King, Paul. 1988. *Risking Liberation: Middle Class Powerlessness and Social Heroism.* Atlanta: John Knox.

O'Neal, Dan, and Alice Blair Wesley, Eds. 1995. *The Transient and Permanent in Liberal Religion: Reflections from the UUMA Convocation on Ministry.* Boston: Skinner House Books.

Rankin, David. 1978. Thoughts following a suicide, in *Portraits From the Cross.* Boston: Unitarian Universalist Association.

Rich, Adrienne, 1978. Power, in *The Dream of a Common Language: Poems 1974–1977.* New York: Norton.

Shaull, Richard. 1984. *Heralds of a New Reformation.* Maryknoll, NY: Orbis.

Tillich, Paul. 1957. *Dynamics of Faith.* New York: Harper & Row.

Wesley, Alice Blair. 1987. *Myths of Time and History: A Unitarian Universalist Theology.* Self-published.

Wilbur, Earl Morse. 1925. *Our Unitarian Heritage.* Boston: Beacon Press.

Wilbur, Earl Morse. 1945. *A History of Unitarianism* (2 volumes). Boston: Beacon Press.

Woodhouse, A.S.P. 1938. *Puritans and Liberty.* London: J. M. Dent & Sons, Ltd.

Wright, Conrad. 1966. *The Beginnings of Unitarianism in North America.* Boston: Beacon Press.

Wright, Conrad. 1997. *Congregational Polity.* Boston: Skinner House Books.

Wright, Conrad. 1989. *Walking Together.* Boston: Skinner House Books.

About the Author

Walter P. Herz, a native of New Rochelle, New York, received his A.B. from Harvard following U.S. Navy service in World War ll. He devoted his business career to medical product marketing with companies in the New York metro area. He specialized in corporate communications including advertising, public and professional relations, and multimedia educational programs. Herz and his spouse Betty joined First Unitarian Church of Plainfield, New Jersey, in 1958. Now, three UU churches and two states later, they belong to First Unitarian Church of Cincinnati. Their two daughters also live in the Cincinnati area.

Over the past forty years, Herz has held virtually every position a UU church has to offer, and by choice he has been denominational affairs chair in all four churches. He has served on the Ohio Valley District Board and is currently the district's Annual Program Fund chair. Herz has written on local UU history for the Cincinnati Historical Society magazine and has published a biography of his maternal grandfather.